TREASURES
OF THE ROYAL BRITISH COLUMBIA MUSEUM AND ARCHIVES

MPORTERS
EXPORTERS

TREA

COMPILED BY JACK LOHMAN

WITH CONTRIBUTIONS FROM

STEVEN POINT

MARTHA BLACK

RICHARD J. HEBDA

GRANT KEDDIE

GARY MITCHELL

SURES

OF THE ROYAL BRITISH COLUMBIA MUSEUM AND ARCHIVES

ROYAL BC MUSEUM
VICTORIA, CANADA

196

CONTENTS

SENĆOŦEN/Malchosen/Lkwungen
Semiahmoo/T'Sou-ke
Nedut'en/Witsuwit'en
Hul'q'umi'num'/Halq'eméylem/hən̓q̓əmin̓əm̓
Oowekyala / 'Uik̓ala
As long as we can protect the landscape, the knowledge is there. It's the landscape and all of the living beings — if we listen to them and to the planet, our languages and our very selves will remain intact.
Competition for lands and resources intensified as the settler population grew. In 1871 Canada prohibited Aboriginal people from fishing commercially and later outlawed traditional fishing methods such as fishing weirs. Industrial resource extraction contaminated and reduced the ecosystems that First Nations depend on for their livelihood. These and other losses of territories and livelihoods compound disruptions to culture and language. First Nations economic development and access to lands and resources are still limited by discriminatory legislation such as the Indian Act.
LOSS OF CHILDREN

INAUGURATED IN 1886 and developed over almost 130 years, the Royal British Columbia Museum marks the achievement of our province's dream of a responsible steward of our collections and archives. The museum boasts exceptional collections representing the people, the natural history and the living cultures of British Columbia. For all of us, it is more than simply a museum; it's a tangible symbol of our pride in our heritage and culture. Over the past few years the museum has succeeded in creating something new and yet something faithful to its traditions. Its new *Our Living Languages* exhibition, created together with the First People's Cultural Council, is an example of partnership, excellence and innovation. As the museum grows, we recognize our joint responsibility to share our collections and the wealth of knowledge contained in them with our province and the world beyond.

I extend my thanks and gratitude to Jack Lohman and his staff on the occasion of the publication of this book.

CORALEE OAKES
British Columbia Minister of Community,
Sport and Cultural Development

INTRODUCTION
ENGAGING THE IMAGINATION

JACK LOHMAN

THE ROYAL BC MUSEUM is an exceptionally rich cross-disciplinary museum created from a large encyclopedic collection and a state archive. It is built on a single underlying concept: the ever-changing diversity of our living and non-living but interconnected world. We speak about the living landscapes and cultures of British Columbia. Our mission emphasizes our passion to engage people in dialogue about the future.

Through diverse exhibitions and diverse audiences, the museum aspires to provide a common ground that acknowledges the complexity of the world we live in. It reaches a multitude of interests, engaging our imagination, our senses, our memory and our capacity to understand and give meaning to the many narratives of our Canadian province.

The museum is a great educator. It offers outstanding learning experiences. Exhibitions, programs, publications and web-based tools are points of departure enriching our understanding of British Columbia and our place within it. Government policy on culture and education is helpful, encouraging the young to get involved.

The museum has traditionally collected, preserved, researched and presented the great heritage of British Columbia. Over time these core functions have evolved and now include other activities. The museum works across the province supporting smaller museums. It is still an avid collector; archives, natural history specimens and works of art are continuously being added to the collections. At the same time, research continues to provide new knowledge about these through scholarly publications and education. Conservators, scientists, curators and collection managers are recognized as contributing to our understanding of all that we steward.

The very size of the museum's collection is daunting. It holds seven million cultural objects and specimens, five historic buildings, several hundred hours of film, five million photographs and some two and a half kilometres of archives. Yet there is never enough to convey a full picture of all the living cultures of British Columbia or to allow an entirely straightforward interpretation of the changing landscapes and history of the province.

The museum's famous dioramas are powerful and evocative. They arouse great curiosity as the wildlife, though it looks so still, is so remarkably alive. It is that direct experience, that unmediated interaction between the visitor and the object, that is at the core of our museum learning. Watch a child in the museum and you see true engagement. They know exactly what they want from the displays and watching them you can sense when their imagination is being engaged. Feelings of delight, curiosity and surprise are immediately apparent. We have so much to learn from them.

As we understand our world better, encounter different cultures with greater frequency, as our audiences and our citizens become more knowledgeable and more discerning, so too does the museum's work. Here research, good design and interpretation play key roles. Interactivity and technology serve to enrich the experience on and off site.

In the following essays and photographs, we explore the core issues behind the museum and celebrate its remarkable work and astonishing collections.

I am indebted to Coralee Oakes, who has consistently encouraged this publication, for her good counsel, warmth and understanding. My gratitude to her is beyond words. But above all I must thank our former board chairs, who clubbed together to make this publication possible: John Walton, John Williams, Donald Hayes and Suromitra Sanatani. To them, the Ministry of Community, Sport and Cultural Development, and Stefan and Magda Opalski, I owe my sincerest thanks.

JACK LOHMAN
Chief Executive Officer

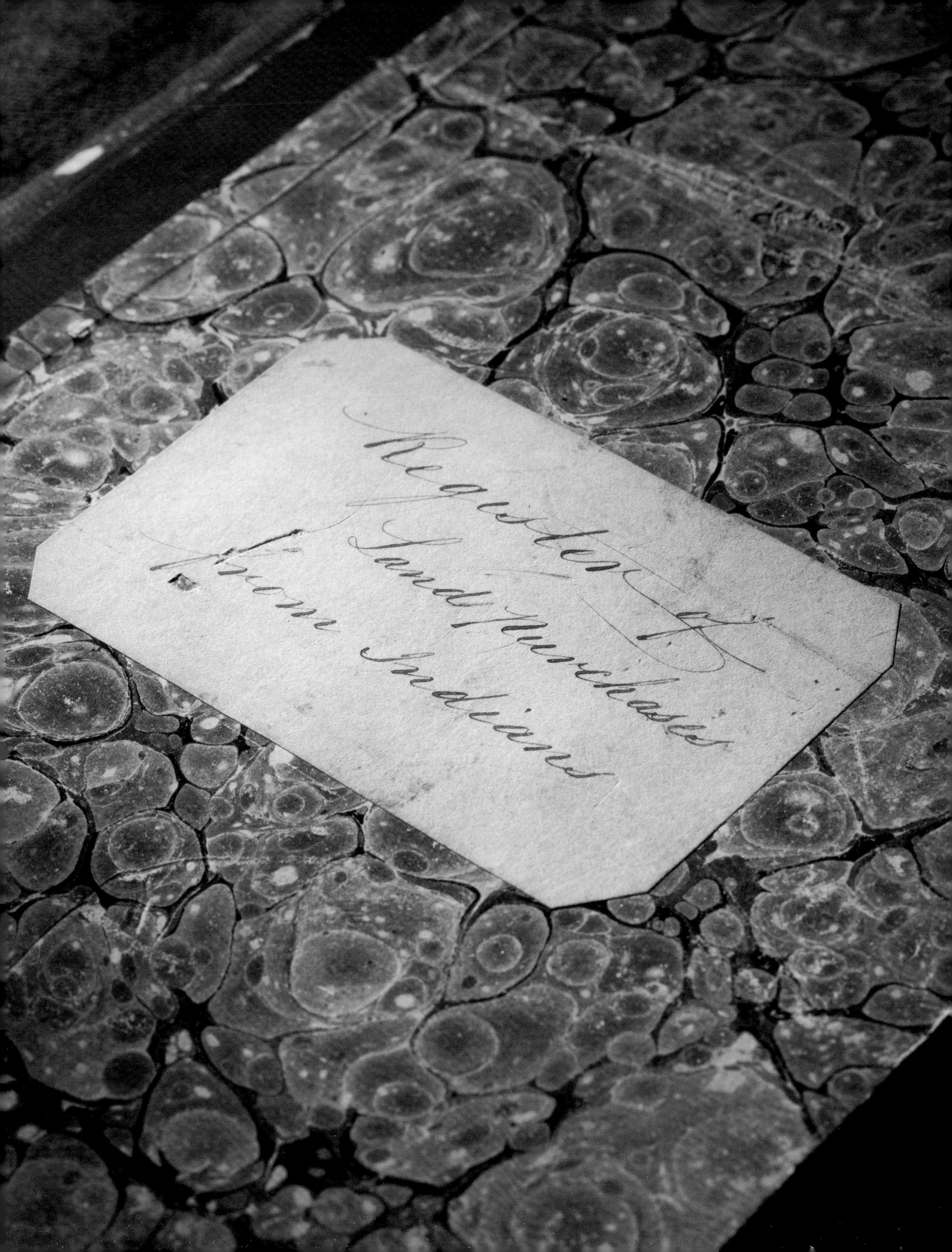
Register of
Land Purchases
from Indians

EMILY CARR

JACK LOHMAN

TRAVELLING BY CARR

NEW WAYS OF REACHING THE INTERIOR

EMILY CARR

FACING: *Roots* by Emily Carr, 1937

IN THE WINTER of 1932, the artist Emily Carr was busy painting portraits. She wrote to her friend Nan Cheney, a medical artist and portrait painter herself, that she was hoping her portraits would help her "get a little green out of my eye."[1]

It is such an artist's thing to say—as though somehow the eye could be caught by what it had seen, invaded by green. But in a landscape like British Columbia's, we know what she means. Throughout her life Carr was overwhelmed (as many of us are) by the greens she encountered on the west coast. Take, for example, a late work by Carr entitled *Roots*. Dark forms surge up in the foreground. And yet just look at how the greens hold their own against those menacing roots. They're not going anywhere. We too have seen those greens: the lush growth, the forests that Emily Carr depicted with elemental force. We see them around us, and we can see them in her paintings.

FACING: Claudia Copley, a senior collections manager in entomology who specializes in spiders, working on a few of the museum's 600,000 insect specimens.

Colour fired Carr's imagination. For this painter of such intensity, it was inseparable from the power of things. In her first book, *Klee Wyck*, we discover (as did the judges who awarded her a Governor General's Award for literature in 1941) that Emily Carr can write as well as she paints. She paddles up to a mission house "stuffed with black."[2] She notices Haida poles along the coast of Skedans Bay "bleached to a pinkish silver colour and cracked by the sun."[3]

Carr's sensitivity to colour is illuminating. And it prompts me to ask: What is it that colours our response to what we see? Is Carr looking for colour—and so she finds it? Or is there something more complex going on, some sense that what surrounds us—in nature, in our environment—is shaping us in the very moment we are shaping it? Our way of thinking is in dialogue with what we see.

What does it mean—in British Columbia, or anywhere really—to have "a little green" in your eye?

Nature

The story of nature is a human story. This may appear to be a contradiction, but I think it's true. As a category of knowledge, nature could be defined as everything that is not afflicted by the touch of human hands. But there is no understanding of nature without our gaze. We consider its variety, we study its evolution, we measure its long prehistory. We predict how nature will outlast us.

One of the curious things about museums is that they are seen to be the antithesis of the natural world. Ask busy shoppers what a museum contains and their first responses are likely to be descriptions of stuffed animals, a model of an old town or a ship, or old artifacts. Tools often feature. These shoppers may not have been in a museum lately, but their impressions remain.

As a museum director, this is a particularly vexing attitude to confront in British Columbia, celebrated as it is for its natural, outdoor beauty. It's as if museums are the opposite of all that glory. And yet, paradoxically, you can come inside the Royal BC Museum and see an astonishing collection of flowers, birds, fish, mammals and reptiles. The collection holds more than 100,000 specimens of vertebrates, 200,000 of plants. And if you have ever been camping in BC, you will not be surprised to hear—we have 600,000 specimens of terrestrial invertebrates: flies, beetles, bees, wasps and, of course, spiders.

You can see many of these things outdoors. But could you ever see so much variety in one place? Rare indeed is the angler who has seen all of the 647 species of fishes you can find in the Royal BC Museum. Birdwatchers are natural list-makers, competitively so. But how many can boast of having spotted all 450 species we have at the museum? Among its many scientific virtues, the Royal BC Museum collection contains fossilized plants and animals, some over 550 million years old. It also contains what are called *type specimens*, the "perfect examples" of species when they are first

identified and described. The very basis of what the world knows of nature is held in the museum stores and is of international importance.

A good example is the Nootka Rose (*Rosa nutkana*). You can find these wild roses up and down the coast of North America, but the specimen reproduced above was picked in Victoria on June 16, 1896, by James R. Anderson. Anderson and his wife gathered botanical specimens across Vancouver Island and many of the Royal BC Museum's oldest examples are from their collections. The specimen has aged beautifully. After almost 120 years, it is reminiscent of a sepia-toned photograph of the 19th century. The Nootka Rose was named after Nootka Sound. When the Bohemian botanist Carl Presl described this species, the plant material he used was collected from Nootka Sound on the west coast of Vancouver Island.

It is a wondrous thing and it keeps a precise body of botanical knowledge safe within its delicate leaves and preserved folds. It also tells us something about British Columbia. If the museum's natural history collections are themselves a vast map of nature in all its forms, the very name of this plant can tell us quite specifically about human history and the maps that men have made. Nootka Sound, after which Presl names a pretty wild rose, can only be called that once someone has named the place or, later, settlers, with a keener interest in property, have defined its borders by law. The Nootka Rose carries within its very name a piece of human history.[4]

Other plants in the collection can tell us other histories. The museum has another of Anderson's harvestings, a Salmonberry (*Rubus spectabilis*) he collected in Goldstream Park, just northwest of Victoria, in 1899. You might think such objects are inert and of little interest any longer. But in May 2012, researchers from Simon Fraser University took leaf impressions from the undersides of this very specimen as well as other examples of Salmonberry in our collection. The scientists are testing the correlation between stomata density on the underside of the leaves and the concentration of carbon dioxide in the atmosphere. This relationship has been demonstrated in laboratory settings and is now being investigated in the wild as a means of documenting the effects of global climate change.

So once again, here is a story of global importance in the museum collection. Because we have preserved such a historical object, scientists today can document environmental change over long spans of time—exactly the sort of data we urgently need. The Royal BC

FACING: A specimen of Nootka Rose (*Rosa nutkana*) collected by botanist J.R. Anderson in 1896. This widespread British Columbia species was named by Bohemian botanist Carl Presl in honour of Nootka Sound.

Museum collection is full of such objects. They document natural history, certainly, such as the evolution of species. But they also tell us of social change, of human impact. Among the stranger guest appearances in the collection is the albino Oscar (*Astronotus ocellatus*), a rather ugly but popular aquarium fish from South America. It was discovered in Chemainus in 2011 and shows us, among other things, the effect the pet trade is having on species distribution.

British Columbia is an outdoor place, but how we get there and what we take with us is very much a product of what has coloured our minds indoors. Once you've seen an albino fish, it is hard not to look for its companion. Once you've learned about the traditional use of plants and animals among the smart ecologies of the First Nations—and yes, you can learn those things in the museum—then your understanding of BC's glorious landscape takes on a whole new meaning, as you walk along the sea wall in Vancouver's Stanley Park or hike the mountainous trails of Logan Pass in Glacier National Park.

To return to our shoppers, cultural bodies like the Royal BC Museum have to compete for their attention. People are often unaware not just of the astonishing collections of natural history we have but of their relevance today. It is in part a question of communicating what museums do. Yes, we preserve knowledge, but it is living knowledge, knowledge that innovative exhibits and books, new forms of media, topical ideas and fresh approaches can animate. If all visitors see is the display case and not the display in all its vital, intellectual force, then inspiration has failed miserably and the collection is not doing all that it could.

There are, alas, all too many examples of this happening. In his first collection of short stories, the Quebec-based writer Neil Bissoondath describes a Canadian narrator both dazzled and dismayed by the art and architecture of Europe, and in particular its museums:

> Endless miles of flying buttresses, crowds of spires and gargoyles: boundless piety carved in stone. And then the museums. I gave up on them early on, all the paintings and statues, centuries and a continent on display, when I began to feel that all of Europe was a museum, and all the men and women merely caretakers; when it began to seem to me that no sooner had Europe lived a passage of its life than it put the relics on display behind glass sombrely labelled, the past—remote and recent—neatly packaged.[5]

Oh those dried-up Europeans. But let's not feel too smug yet. Canadian museums, at least those in eastern Canada, fare no better with our young backpacker, James. Bissoondath writes:

> It is, I realize, the same sensation that comes to me after a few hours spent in the Royal Ontario Museum or the Art Gallery: enough of the old and the captured; time needed to assimilate it, store it; and time, then, to breathe the fresher air of things yet uninvented.[6]

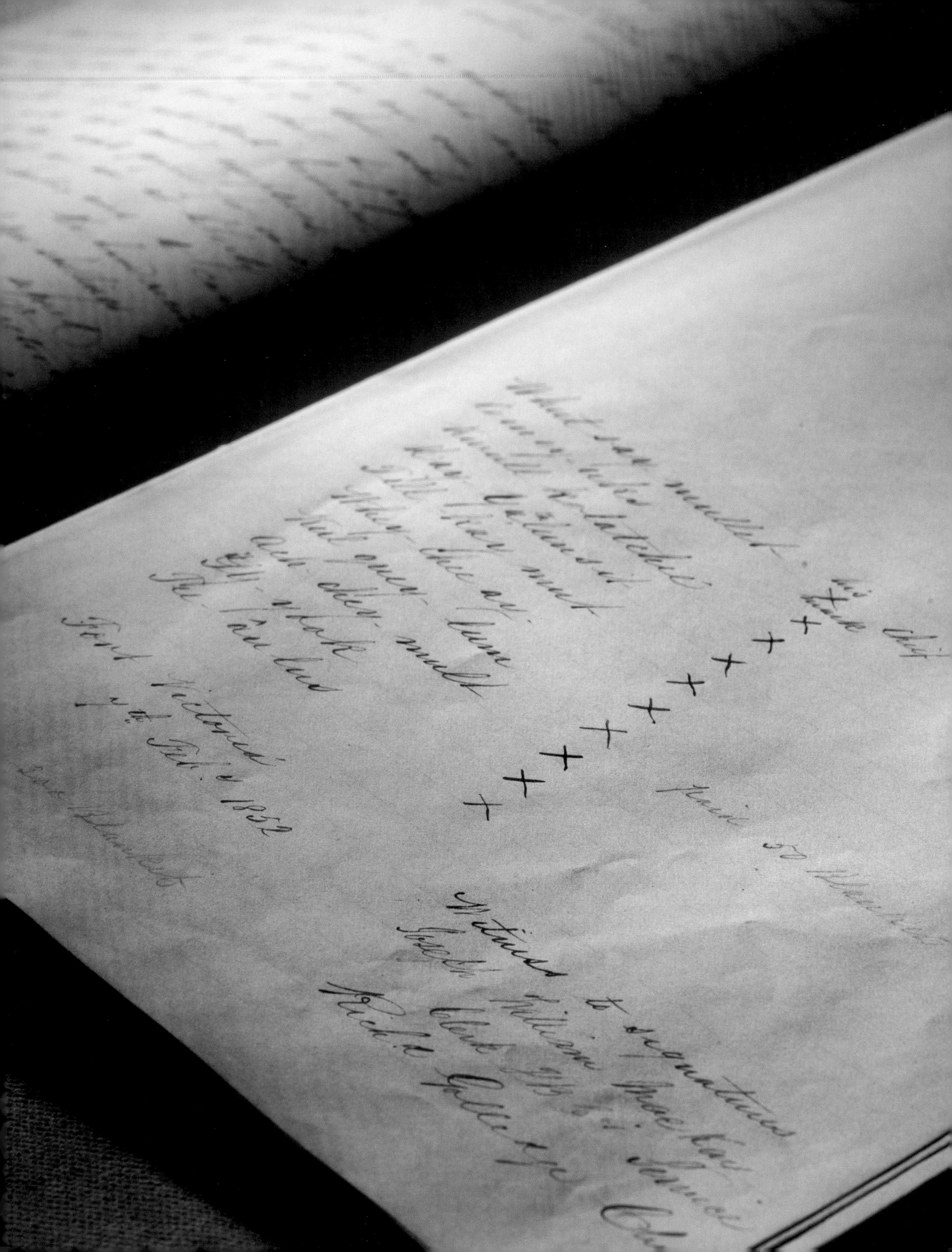
Fort Victoria
1st Feb. 1852
Witness to signatures

FACING: A page from one of the 14 "Douglas Treaties," 1852, one of the first and only land agreements signed by British Columbia's First Nations; the cover is shown on page 23.

The very size of the museum's collection is daunting. It holds seven million cultural objects and specimens, five historic buildings, several hundred hours of film, five million photographs and some two and a half kilometres of archives. Yet there is never enough to convey a full picture of all the living cultures of British Columbia.

JACK LOHMAN

FACING: The Turnagain Nugget, a 1.6-kilogram chunk of gold found in 1937 by Alice Shea. The nugget got its name because Shea spied it in the Turnagain River in BC's far north.

I will come back to the "uninvented," but let's just pause and remind young James that unlike Ben Stiller, he need not spend the night in the museum.[7] Much as we appreciate his attendance, that was never our intention. The whole point is to do just what he plans: to store, to assimilate, to go back outside and into one's life challenged. Changed. Breathing deeper. Richer for having been inside.

History

Did you know that "Victoria, British Columbia, is the best place to fit out and sail from"? And what's more: "All steamboats going North start out from or call at Victoria." The reason? A newspaper ad of the late 1890s provides the answer: "Klondyke Gold Fields are in Canada!"

If nature is the first great topic of BC and the Royal BC Museum, then history is surely a close second. As I hope I've shown, there is no natural history without human history. What we know of nature comes from the human eye casting forth to understand what has been and what it can see. One of the great strengths of the Royal BC Museum's combination of natural and historical collections is that, together, they give us history in its fullest span. The paleontology collections take us back millennia. They can show visitors how BC is one of the most fascinating geological settings on earth. When ancient island terranes and the rocky ocean floor collided with the North American continent, they created mountains. It's hard to envisage, but the museum can get all of us, children and adults alike, to imagine a time *before* the mountains were there. It's unnerving.

Of course, more recent history, the history of mankind, is not a separate topic from nature, and one of the things the Royal BC Museum needs to do better is integrate these stories. What British Columbian could imagine their life divorced from the landscape? The land itself changes human history. Without BC's natural resources, there would be no gold rushes, no hydro-electric power, no forestry or fisheries. Fossils tell us not just about past life forms, but have a modern-day function: they can indicate geologically where petroleum and minerals might be found. That influence (of nature benefitting people) turns the other way when it is human behaviour that changes the land. When economists and environmentalists wage war over the laying of pipelines to transport oil, one of the effects they need to measure is the cost to BC's environment and its despoliation.

The Royal BC Museum has some astonishing artifacts that bring history to life. Delve into the archives and you can find an original Vancouver Island treaty signed in 1850. You can see the names of the newcomers, and those of the First Nations chiefs, whose signatures are already so alien to the process that they appear as a column of meaningless Xs. It's an important and troubling document. Phrases such as "becomes the entire property of the white people forever" tend to leap out for the visitor.

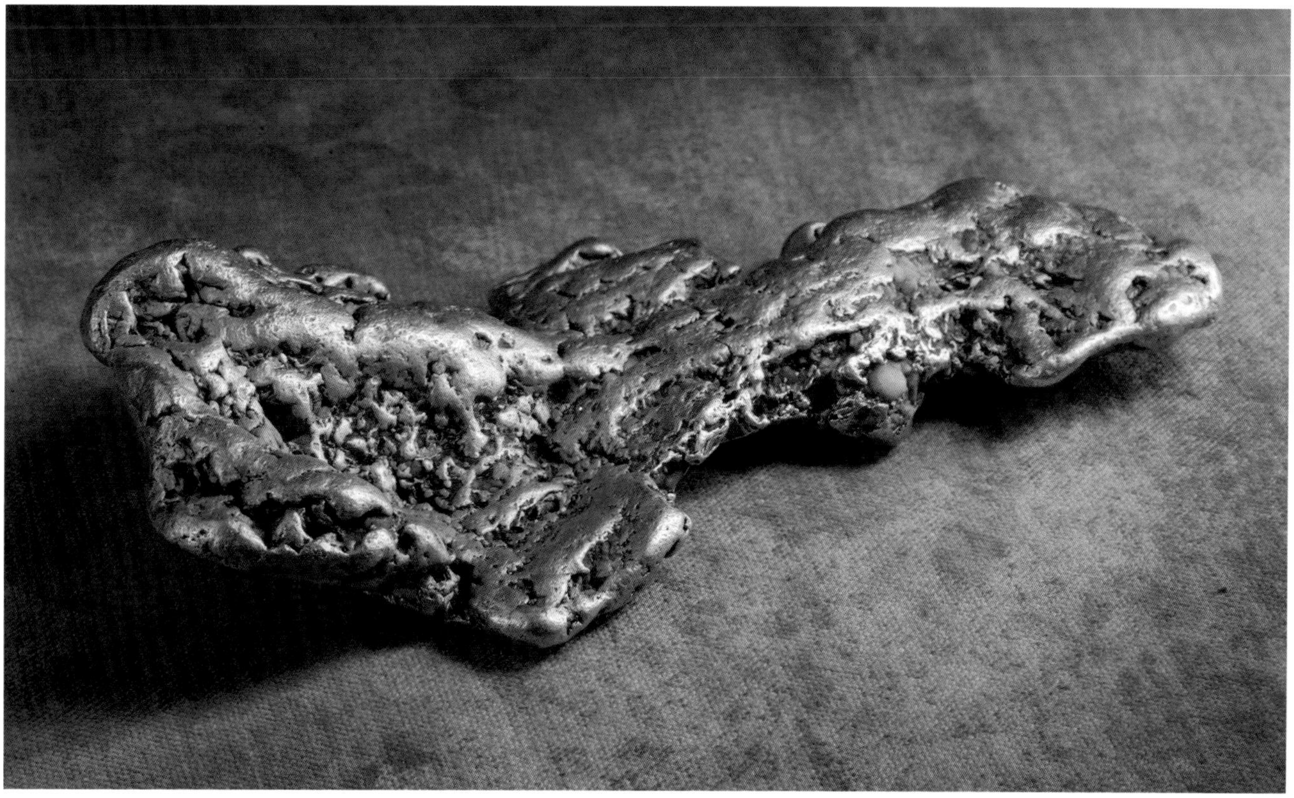

The treaty is living history. It is a voice that speaks directly from the past. But it is not the most photogenic item. Instead, the golden box pictured overleaf might fire your imagination. On the lid of this box is a Killer Whale leaping through the air. Beaver and humans are depicted on the base. It is, as you might guess from the design, a work by one of Canada's most celebrated artists, Bill Reid. The Royal BC Museum contains 17 of Reid's works, including a Western Redcedar screen carved with crouching figures and powerful animals. It is a great sculpture in which man and nature intertwine, and I am proud to say that it was specially commissioned by the museum in 1968.

The box, like all of Reid's works, is a springboard for any number of fascinating stories. Most important is its connection to the Haida people. Reid's mother's family came from Haida Gwaii (the Queen Charlotte Islands), and Reid's life became a commitment to understanding and celebrating Haida culture.

As with many objects, we can choose what story we want to tell. We could talk about spirit tales and religion. We could talk about the natural world, how it inspires us, how we record it. One of the things you'll notice is that the box is made of 22-carat gold. Reid was a printmaker. He worked in wood and silver. Why did he choose gold for this box? Here, the material evokes another important story in BC's past, that of the gold rush. Those Klondike gold fields I mentioned earlier are a silent backdrop to Reid's choice of material. But they shouldn't be. This is what museums are good at. We can encourage visitors to make these connections, to leap over time like a Killer Whale, to weave a rich tapestry of history out of a single display.

FACING: Haida box by Bill Reid, 1971, made of cast, hammered and engraved gold.

The Klondike gold fields are a silent backdrop to Bill Reid's choice of gold as a material. This is what museums are good at—we can encourage visitors to make these connections, to leap over time like a Killer Whale, to weave a rich tapestry of history out of a single display.

JACK LOHMAN

Freight wagons and mule teams on the Cariboo Road, photographed by Frederick Dally in 1867–68. Englishman Dally produced some of the most iconic images of gold-rush BC during a brief and prolific career behind the camera (1866–70).

And there is rich history to mine here. Not just of what people might know of the gold rushes that shaped British Columbia, but of the many lost histories that need to be foregrounded. Traditional history kept these stories separate. But one of the histories we need to integrate is how the First Nations were involved in the discovery of gold. Another would be the story of immigrant labour. Chinese workers were among those who arrived in large numbers, and who would remain long after the rush for gold ceased.[8]

The Chinese would change the culture of the west coast. The museum has a Chinese Freemasons' lantern (pictured on pages 4 and 124) that shows evidence of this rich seam of BC life. It was made between 1910 and 1930, and is the oldest running-horse lantern we know of from any of Canada's Chinatowns. It is made of paper over a metre-tall bamboo frame, and the heat from lights or candles powered an intricate system of wheels and strands of hair that moved parts of the lantern. I can't tell you how enchanting it is. Horsemen hail as they ride past. A caterpillar unfurls itself. Squirrels chomp nuts. Crabs wave their pincers.

ABOVE: *British Columbia Miners, 1864*, by William Hind, an English-born painter who created many colourful images of the Cariboo gold rush.

Of course the gold rush is a story all its own, and we may even need to cast our cultural eye more widely than what fits inside the museum. The Cariboo Wagon Road—the very conduit of the spirit of the gold rush—is still there and is a potential attraction all its own for tourism, certainly, and as a cultural benefit for all. I am keen to promote this gold route as one of the world's great stories of immigration, innovation and change. And the Royal BC Museum can illuminate that story. Did you know that camels were brought up from the United States to travel to the interior? We have in our collection the very shoes used to protect their hooves from the Canadian snow, and we have saddles, maps and prospectors' information. The 19th-century photographer Frederick Dally hauled heavy glass plates into northern BC. He selected his precious camera shots with immense care, so few could he make. Those stunning photographs are in the Royal BC Museum (you can see an example on page 38).

The point is, ultimately, that a museum like the Royal BC Museum can inspire understanding not just of the landscape, but of the story of people in that landscape. And that's our story. It is nearly 150 years since Canadian Confederation, and we should be celebrating a long history. Stop feeling like newcomers on the world stage. Canada's is a proud story of what became of the world here. Of the rich mix we have today. Of what this museum can show you: everything from camel shoes to Haida gold.

Art

What I would like us to do, in essence, is think big: of long histories and world impacts, and of the stupendous natural grandeur that inspires us every day. The large scale is one of the things that attracts visitors' attention—think of the Egyptian pyramids, the Eiffel Tower, Angkor Wat. Who is better placed to take on the "big" than British Columbia, with its vast ocean, its tall forests, its soaring mountains? We are surrounded by "big."

Museums miss a trick by ignoring the scale outdoors. We mustn't cower. We must embrace it. One of the earliest First Nations poles to come into the Royal BC Museum in the 1890s was a house post from Haida Gwaii (see photo on page 57). It came from Chief Nestaqana's dwelling, a building whose name in the Haida language translates as "House So Large That People Must Shout To Make Themselves Heard In It."[9]

FACING: Tzu-I Chung, curator of history at the Royal BC Museum, a specialist in the intercultural history of the province.

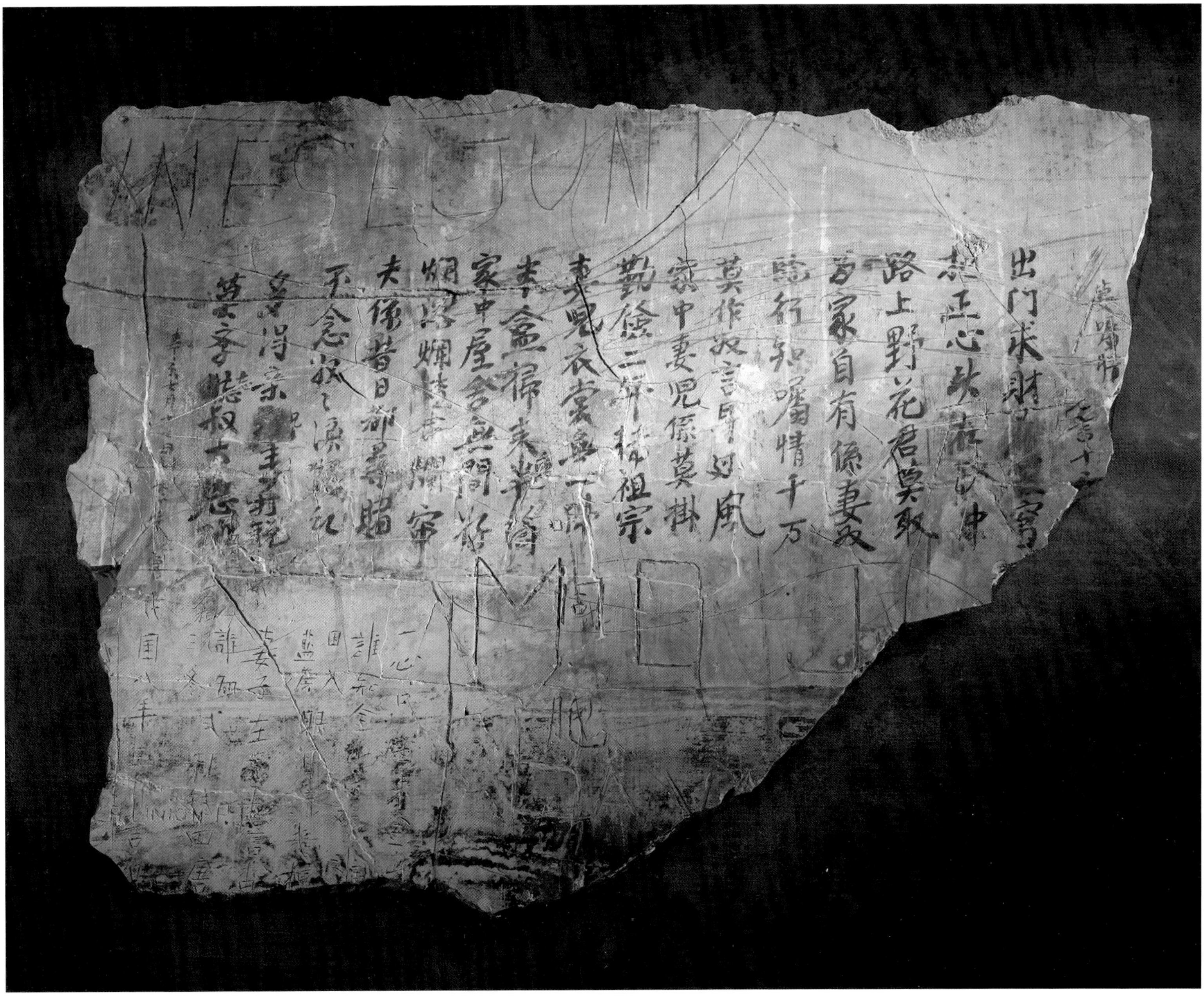

ABOVE: "My Wife's Admonishment," a melancholy poem scratched on the wall of Victoria's immigration building by a newly arrived Chinese immigrant, 1911; it begins, "You go abroad to seek wealth because we are poor. / In your sojourn, you do not sow your wild oats."

That's big! It makes sense in a natural setting, and if we design our museum well, it makes sense in the collection. This impressive pole is a part of history not left to decay outdoors, but preserved to record the past, and honour the Haida people who made it.

The main figure is another Killer Whale. After the whale abducted his wife, the hero Nanasimgit journeyed to its house under the sea to rescue her. This intriguing tale and the pole's authority express something the painter Emily Carr once wrote about during a visit to a Kwakwaka'wakw village: "The power I felt was not in the thing itself, but in some tremendous force behind it that the carver had believed in."[10] What the pole conveys is cultural force, and if museums can recreate that force, visitors will find other cultural artifacts, however small, however incidental, much more vivid. The story we tell in the museum is partly about getting people to feel the past, not just look at it.

FACING: One of the devices used by ethnomusicologist Ida Halpern to record and play the traditional songs of British Columbia First Nations, particularly the Kwakwa̱ka̱'wakw, in the mid 20th century; a disc can be seen on page 133.

One of the ways we can do that is through sound. Intangible heritage is a growing area of study worldwide. How do you keep track of cultural expressions that do not take the form of things? How do you record practices transmitted down the generations? The Royal BC Museum holds 700,000 hours of recorded sound. It is not the first thing people think of when they imagine a museum's collection. But it's there, and it includes such treasures as Ida Halpern's collection of First Nations songs, which she first began to record in the 1940s. The tapes have an immediacy no one interested in the past would wish to be without. The museum is currently digitizing the songs, to preserve them but also so that anyone can access them.

In 2012 the UN published its first study on tourism and intangible cultural heritage. Museums don't exist in a vacuum and knowing how we participate in the wider economy is one of our many responsibilities to the government and the public. As the UN has shown, in a world of mass tourism, intangible heritage is a big draw. Gastronomy, street festivals, music—it even includes what the UN calls "knowledge and practices concerning nature." This is, I would argue, particularly relevant in British Columbia, where traditional knowledge of the land has often been lost or overlooked. BC has the highest number of animal and plant species of any province in Canada. We worry on the one hand about the disappearance of salmon and eulachon, cedar and bear, and yet we do nowhere near enough to promote understanding nature.

One of the Canadians we can learn from is that great painter of nature, Emily Carr. The Royal BC Museum contains Carr's professional and personal records, along with more than 1000 works of art. They span her entire career. They include notebooks, major paintings in oil and watercolour, drawings, cartoons, works in fabric and clay. Carr is a Canadian icon. Her works hang in all of Canada's major galleries. In 2014 the Royal BC Museum loaned 25 items to England's Dulwich Picture Gallery for a major international exhibition on Carr.

Is she celebrated? In my opinion, not nearly enough, and the Royal BC Museum's planned new *Emily Carr* gallery is going to change all that. Stay tuned! There are so many facets of her work we can learn from, and this is in part because she gets us to appreciate the natural world by taking us in and out of the museum (rather like our cultural attention to gold rushes might move from camel shoes to the Cariboo Road). Take the archival image of Carr sketching at Tanu[11] on Haida Gwaii in 1912, reproduced overleaf. It is an amazing photograph. It's as if Carr were plunked down all alone and given an entire land to concentrate on. She is not indoors, but outdoors. Reading *Klee Wyck* and her later books, you get that sense—that what Carr needed more than anything was to absorb the world around her.

Compare this photograph to the painting she produced a year later, facing it on page 45. It too is in the museum, and it is just this sort of interconnection that makes the Carr collection so compelling. We have

a historical photograph of the great painter in a specific place. And we have her painting of that very scene, no longer a colourless photograph, but transformed in rich oil paints: layered in greens and blues, precisely marked in reds. It's as if we're allowed to see her, to see what she saw—and then to see it through her eyes.

It is this relationship between the world and our creative minds that is at the heart of the Royal BC Museum. Any artifact, like Carr's painting, can teach us how to see. It reminds us of what is there—the natural world, the people who inhabit the land—and at the same time, it celebrates what is not there, the uninvented, the particular lens any of us might bring to seeing what surrounds us. When I first saw Emily Carr's paintings, I thought she'd made up the colours, they were so vivid, so strong, as her style developed throughout the 1930s. Then I looked out the window of my office and off the balcony of my apartment. And I saw that Emily Carr was a realist.

The colours of Emily Carr are just one exact and very fine example of how museum artifacts reflect the world. You can find the world in them, but look closely and they will shift your understanding of what you see.

So I know what Carr meant when she felt she had "a little green in her eye." She may have meant nature itself. She may have meant her paintings. But as for me, I've got Nootka Rose, Haida gold, more than 1000 Carrs. When I go looking inside and beyond the museum, I've got the entire spectrum.

FACING: Artist Emily Carr sketching at t'anuu 'llnagaay (Tanoo or Tanu) in 1912. Carr visited Haida Gwaii as part of a six-week trip dedicated to visiting First Nations villages and making images of aboriginal art in context.

BELOW: *Tanoo, Queen Charlotte Islands, B.C.*, a large oil painting by Emily Carr from 1913. T'anuu 'llnagaay (Tanoo or Tanu) was abandoned in the 1880s and many of the poles were later removed, some to be conserved in the Royal BC Museum (see photo page 67).

ABOVE: *Seascape* by Emily Carr, 1933.

FACING: *Haida Totems, Cha-Atl, Queen Charlotte Islands,* a watercolour by Emily Carr from 1912.

M.EMILY CARR. 1912

MARTHA BLACK

LIVING CULTURES

FROM ARTIFACTS TO PARTNERSHIPS

FACING: Kwakwa̱ka̱'wakw masks in Nawalagwatsi, the Cave of Supernatural Power, *First Peoples* gallery.

WHEN IT WAS founded in 1886 in response to a citizens' petition, there were just two collection areas in British Columbia's provincial museum: natural history specimens and Aboriginal artifacts. The conjunction of natural and Aboriginal collections reflects colonial attitudes to First Nations as separate from contemporary society and modern culture, as well as the equation of anthropology with the natural sciences. Just as understanding the natural environments of the province involved the discovery, naming and classification of native plants and animals, the understanding of native peoples required naming and classification according to 19th-century anthropological categories. First Nations "artifacts" acquired for private and museum collections were removed physically from their places of origin and conceptually from their original meanings. A European intellectual structure erased these contexts and replaced them with categories and nomenclatures of European epistemology.

Part of the work of museums that have inherited these collections is to recognize and dismantle the imposed structure, and learn from First Nations people today about past and present meanings of the museum objects and what they can mean in the future. We come to understand the objects as active agents, not passive collections documenting a "primitive" past. This learning, which can only be done through collaborations with First Nations, involves transfer of interpretive authority and possibly physical transfer of objects to First Nations.

British Columbia's Provincial Museum of Natural History and Anthropology was founded in the late 19th century during the great age of museum anthropology. Many of the museums established in this period began in response to existing collections. (The Field Museum in Chicago, for example, was built to house collections from the World's Columbian Exposition of 1893.) BC's museum was different: it began, not to house a collection of First Nations artifacts, but to start one.

After about 1880 there was an enormous appetite for First Nations artifacts, particularly dramatic ceremonial and "exotic" objects from the Northwest Coast. Collectors working on behalf of American and European museums competed to acquire the best—which usually meant old and, therefore, "authentic"—examples and shipped tons of material out of the province. The Victoria *Daily Colonist* newspaper reported on October 15, 1885, that "Professor Jacobsen and his brother" (the collectors Johan Adrian Jacobsen and Bernard Fillip Jacobsen) departed for Berlin with "nine Indians from the west coast of the Bella Bella tribe" (actually, they were Nuxalk from Bella Coola) and "several tons of curios… which cost over $4,000." The article noted that Adrian Jacobsen "has purchased and shipped from this coast in all about $10,000 worth of Indian curios," a considerable sum at the time.

Prominent citizens of Victoria were concerned about the loss of this heritage, which they saw as belonging to the province, and formally petitioned the lieutenant governor for a museum in Victoria. "It has long been felt desirable that a Provincial Museum should be established in order to preserve specimens of the natural products and Indian Antiquities and Manufactures of the Province and to classify and exhibit the same for the information of the public," they wrote. The petition was favourably received and the Royal BC Museum is its legacy. We see things differently now, however.

Aboriginal collections subsequently acquired by this museum reflect the perspectives of the collectors and their fluctuating budgets. This meant that acquisitions were frequently inconsistent and unsystematic; over time, they also reveal changing attitudes toward artifacts and, by extension, to First Peoples in BC.

The nine Nuxalk men who went to Germany with Adrian and Fillip Jacobsen in 1885 are pictured on this *carte de visite* advertising a Victoria store specializing in First Nations curios.

Anonymous Sources (1890s)

The collectors' descriptions of the museum's earliest ethnographic acquisitions reflect anthropological attitudes and romantic cultural generalizations of the time. Collections made by James Deans and Fillip Jacobsen, which the museum purchased in 1893, shed light on what was still available to collectors despite the great quantities of artifacts that had been removed from Northwest Coast communities in the previous decade. They also illustrate the type of information that collectors were able to access and what they thought was appropriate to record for museum documentation. From our modern viewpoint, these records are frustratingly minimal and uninformative. Today we would like to know the specifics of the transactions. How did the collectors obtain these objects? Who did they come from? What were their circumstances? If sold, as most were, how were the prices arrived at? What are the objects' histories, their correct names, their uses, their connections to the lineages?

In contrast to the interactions that interest us today, collectors like James Deans and Fillip Jacobsen—neither of whom had any training as anthropologists—wrote down information they thought anthropologists and museums would want. Both had been commissioned by Franz Boas to collect Northwest Coast material for the 1893 World's Columbia Exposition (the Chicago World's Fair) and were influenced by the "objective" anthropological agenda, even though, as residents of BC, they must have had a more local perspective.

The Royal BC Museum is a place where changes are both mirrored and initiated. We have learned from the patient, and often not so patient, demands by First Nations for inclusion in the museum and authority over the interpretation of the objects from their ancestors and communities.

—— MARTHA BLACK

Deans and Jacobsen were trying to capture cultures as they were in the past. Today we would like to know about the cultures as they were in Deans' and Jacobsen's time—their present. We now foreground interactions; collaborations and partnerships with First Nations are the norm. For Deans, Jacobsen and other artifact collectors of the 19th century, the dynamics of encounter had no place in the record and the sources of the artifacts were anonymous ciphers of a disappearing way of life.

Collection from James Deans

James Deans (1827–1905) came from Scotland in 1853 to work on Hudson's Bay Company farms in southern Vancouver Island and settled in Victoria after his contract ended. He travelled often to Haida Gwaii, first as an employee of the Queen Charlotte Coal Company from 1869 to 1872, and then as a collector of Haida artifacts for several museums. In 1892 Franz Boas commissioned him to collect Haida material for the World's Fair, and Deans went with the Kwakwa̱ka̱'wakw delegation to the Chicago exhibition. (It is reported that the Kwakwa̱ka̱'wakw thought him overbearing and rude.[1]) Deans was an active member of the Natural History Society of British Columbia, which was affiliated with the provincial museum, and in 1890 presented papers titled *The Preservation of the Indian Remains of BC*, *The Haidah Legend of the Mountain Goat* and *Certain Myths of the Queen Charlotte Islanders*. His book of Haida legends, *Tales from the Totems of Hidery*, was published in 1899. By all accounts, Deans was a self-styled authority whom some considered a rather eccentric amateur. When asked in 1911 for an opinion about the catalogue of a collection purchased by the Geological Society of Canada in 1898 from a Victoria artifact dealer, Charles F. Newcombe wrote that it was done by Deans "mostly from guess work" and implied that the information was not worth much.[2]

The first two entries in the Royal BC Museum's ethnology catalogue, a pair of Haida house posts from hlragilda 'llnagaay (Skidegate), are part of a collection that Deans made on Haida Gwaii in 1892 and sold to the museum for $298 the following year. A comparison of the old catalogue entry with a recent description of one of these house posts highlights changing conventions. The current description is based on information from scholars such as George MacDonald and Robin Wright, who base their research on both historical documentation and contemporary Haida knowledge:

> This house post stood at the back of a dwelling belonging to Chief Nestaqana of the Big House People lineage of the Eagle division of the Haida. The name of the house, which refers to its great size, can be translated as House So Large That People Must Shout To Make Themselves Heard In It. There are several possible interpretations of the images on this post. One is that the top figure is Raven with a broken beak and the other figures illustrate the story

A house post photographed by Richard Maynard at hlragilda 'llnagaay (Skidegate), Haida Gwaii, 1884. The pole was acquired by the museum in 1893 and is now in the *First Peoples* gallery.

> of Nanasimgit. Nanasimgit's wife, who can be identified by the labret in her lower lip, was abducted by a Killer Whale. Nanasimgit journeyed to the Killer Whale's undersea house and rescued her. The main image on the pole represents the Killer Whale.

Contrast the information about the same pole in the museum's old catalogue entry, no doubt based on information from Deans: "This column stood inside the house of the principal chief at Skidegate; the figures are a raven image, a bear and perhaps dogfish or sea monster." The entry for the other post from the same house says, "it was made by one of the Edenshaw's of Masset." Did Deans not know what the figures were, which member of the Edenshaw family carved one or both of the poles, the name of the chief who owned the house, the house's location in the village, and the seller's name? Today we understand intangible heritage to be an integral part of an object, one that connects it to living culture. For Deans, the "story" the artifacts told was different and continuity between past and present was unknown, misunderstood or deliberately obscured.

Deans' collection is evenly divided between older objects that were used in Haida contexts and newer carvings, including carved figures: a chief in regalia, male and female shamans, and two figures representing the "spirit of death." Were these models commissioned by Deans for the museum or were they standard productions for the artifact trade? Were the shaman and death-spirit figures considered museum worthy because they portrayed exotic remnants of a primitive past? Who were the carvers? And did Deans, in fact, purchase all the Haida material on Haida Gwaii? The catalogue entry for a carved "medicine man" says, mysteriously, that it was "picked up in Beacon Hill Park," Victoria. For us today, the methods and contexts of acquisition are integral to the object. For Deans, the objects spoke for themselves. It appears that he read them as colourful illustrations of exotic primitive cultures of the past.

PRECEDING PAGES and FACING: The interior of the Jonathan Hunt House, a Kwakwa̲ka̲'wakw house in the *First Peoples* gallery. The facing photo shows a detail of a house post carved by Tony Hunt.

Collection from Bernard Fillip Jacobsen

The other collection that the provincial museum purchased in 1893 is arguably the most significant museum collection anywhere of Heiltsuk and Nuxalk cultural material. And the information provided with it is even more frustratingly minimal than that of Deans.[3]

Bernard Fillip Jacobsen (1864–1935) was a Norwegian entrepreneur, farmer and artifact collector based in Bella Coola. He had come to British Columbia in 1884 as an agent for Carl Hagenbeck, a Hamburg importer and exhibitor of exotic wild animals who had a sideline arranging exhibitions of Aboriginal people, such as Lapps and Inuit, in Germany. Hagenbeck hired Jacobsen to collect artifacts and animal specimens and to arrange for a group of Northwest Coast First Nations people to go on tour in Europe.

In the ethnographic business, Jacobsen was following his older brother, Johan Adrian Jacobsen, who had worked for Hagenbeck in Germany and travelled around BC and Alaska from 1881 to 1883 and through Siberia and Russia in 1884 collecting thousands of artifacts for the Royal Ethnographical Museum in Berlin. Adrian joined Fillip in BC in 1885 and the brothers hired nine Nuxalk people to go with them to Europe. After the Nuxalk tour (which lasted more than a year), Fillip returned to BC and eventually settled at Bella Coola. Artifact collecting continued to be an interest and source of income. His obituary in Victoria's *Daily Colonist* newspaper noted: "During his long residence in British Columbia he gathered a remarkable collection of Indian drawings, artifacts and dancing masks, as well as set down scores of Indian legends."

By 1893, when he sold a large collection to the Provincial Museum of Natural History and Anthropology, Jacobsen was familiar with the technologies and ceremonies of the central coast. He shared some of this knowledge with a reporter for the *Daily Colonist* who visited the Indian Department of the museum shortly after Jacobsen's collection had been installed. Jacobsen explained how First Peoples used the tools and utensils, feast dishes and a dance robe in the exhibition. He told the reporter that the "Indians have upwards of sixty distinct dances" and revealed the subjects of some of the masks, including "the Indian who first brought the dance to the O-wee-kanos [Wuikinuxv] . . . the Devil of the River, who capsizes the canoes . . . Raven, who first brought sun to the earth . . . wolf heads [that] each have their own tradition . . . a grizzly bear [that] is given the credit of having provided the fertile valleys . . . crying spirits, before whose time tears were unknown . . . the Goddess of the Seas . . . [and] the Kajul, who brought the dance to the coast. . . ." He recounted the "story of Ianis [*tánís*] the Man-eater and of Nullem-killa [*nułam*] the Dog-eater," explained how Wakas, an 'Isdaítxv chief, acquired the first *tánís* and *nułam* ceremonies and pointed out the masks that represented the spirits of those dances.[4] Jacobsen was speaking from experience: on January 8, 1935, he wrote to Charles Newcombe that he had seen "the Man Eating dance... dozens of times up to 1888" and the "Thunder Bird Dance... ever so many times."[5]

But very little of this knowledge accompanied the artifacts to the provincial museum. The newspaper report concludes with the observation: "Every article has its own interesting story; for which, however, in the absence of catalogue or description of any kind, the visitor must draw mainly upon his imagination." This observation can be applied to the old museum catalogue as well. There are hints of the ceremonial associations. For example, RBCM 72 is described as a Bella Bella "Tlaolacha" (*dhuw'láxᵛa*) mask, but very little of the rich cultural context of the collection is evident. From our current perspective, this information would be central to meaning, but Jacobsen either neglected to provide his understandings for the catalogue or did not consider them relevant in the museological context of the objects. Both Jacobsen and the museum staff comfortably separated tangible heritage and intangible heritage. Today, we understand them to be indivisibly intertwined.

The Jacobsen brothers' early association with the Berlin museum must have given them some understanding of the current scientific standards in ethnology and may account for the composition of their collections. Adrian Jacobsen's 1881–83 collection for Berlin's Royal Ethnographical Museum was biased toward the old and the traditional.[6] Reflecting the museum scholars' interest in "primitive" cultures, Adrian looked for objects that illustrated an ancient way of life and

was particularly interested in old bone and stone artifacts, and religious and ceremonial material. Similarly, Fillip Jacobsen's collection of approximately 222 pieces for BC's provincial museum is biased toward old artifacts that conformed to—and, in the museum setting, created—ideas about authenticity and tradition.

Today we would very much like to know where and from whom Fillip Jacobsen got the objects in this important collection. The lack of information is particularly frustrating because Jacobsen seems to have known quite a lot about what he had acquired.

FACING: Heiltsuk mask and ceremonial puppet, *First Peoples* gallery.

As a central-coast resident involved with the Nuxalk's European tour, he must have been familiar with the communities of Bella Bella and Bella Coola, too. So the minimal documentation about sources is perplexing. Consider, for example, the house entrance pole that Jacobsen purchased from a chief at Old Bella Bella ('Q́élc) at McLoughlin Bay. The figures on the pole are Raven and a sea monster, according to Jacobsen. At one time the pole would have stood at the centre of a traditional house front; the arch at the bottom of the pole was the door to the house. But the pole does not appear in any of the photographs of 'Q́élc. Had it been taken down and stored inside one of the old houses years before Jacobsen acquired it? Or was the chief who sold it at 'Q́élc and the pole in another location? In style, it is closer to Nuxalk poles from Talio and Bella Coola than to the few poles known to come from 'Q́élc. Could it have originated in one of the other Heiltsuk communities, possibly an 'Isdaítxv village, with lineage ties to a Nuxalk community, and taken to 'Q́élc when its owner moved there? RBCM 3 is the only extant house frontal pole that is identified as Heiltsuk. From our modern perspective, Jacobsen's cursory commentary constitutes a further alienation of the pole from its origins.

Seeing Individuals (Early 20th Century)

In the early 20th century, names of First Nations people and communities enter collections documentation in a new way, suggesting a more informed understanding of the connections between cultural objects and living societies. Aboriginal people ceased to be portrayed as symbols of past cultures and were increasingly acknowledged as participants in modern cultures with long, complex histories and established legal systems. With recognition of owners and ownership came a new understanding of the museum's custodial responsibilities. Two significant collections illustrate changing attitudes and approaches to collecting during this period.

Collection from Dr Charles F. Newcombe

Charles Frederick Newcombe (1851–1924) of Victoria was a prolific artifact collector who worked on commission for many museums and maintained a wide network of contacts throughout North America and Europe. From 1895, when he first went to Haida Gwaii, to 1924, when he died in Victoria after a collecting trip to Alert Bay, Newcombe gathered thousands of artifacts. He assembled Haida material for the American Museum of Natural History in New York, made a large collection (some of it obtained from Jacobsen) for the Field Museum in Chicago, and collected for the Geological Survey of Canada, the University of Pennsylvania Museum, the Brooklyn Museum and the Milwaukee Public Museum. Objects from Newcombe are in the Royal Ontario Museum, the Canadian Museum of History, the British Museum, the Peabody Museum of Anthropology and Archaeology at Harvard, the National Museum of Natural History, and museums in Edinburgh, Sydney, Melbourne, Bremen and

many other cities. He was in touch with scores of people involved in all aspects of the artifact trade. Although known primarily as an ethnographic collector, Newcombe was a naturalist and a dedicated collector of botanical specimens, too.

Newcombe is strongly identified with the Royal BC Museum but was only briefly a member of its staff. In 1895 he accompanied museum employee Francis Kermode on a trip to Haida Gwaii and the following year was acting curator in the absence of John Fannin. When the museum's collection was installed in the east wing of the new legislative buildings in 1898, Newcombe was paid $330 to compile a preliminary catalogue and in 1909 was asked to rearrange the ethnographic collection according to language group rather than object types. An illustrated catalogue, *Guide to the Anthropological Collection in the Provincial Museum*, was the result. Despite his sporadic formal associations with the institution, though, Newcombe was a major influence and arguably "played as large a part in the history of the museum as any of its directors."[7]

The continuing removal of artifacts to distant collections continued to be a concern, so in 1911 the province provided Newcombe with funds to expand the museum's collection of First Nations material. By this time, BC's economy was booming and First Nations people were being pushed to the sidelines, a situation that, as Douglas Cole observes, contributed to the provincial government's renewed interest in securing a representative collection of First Nations material culture before it disappeared: "The native Indians were regarded as increasingly irrelevant to the rapidly developing province.... Less than ever a nuisance or an obstacle to progress, native arts could be more readily appreciated."[8]

Paradoxically, the declining First Nations presence in the socio-political realm contrasts with their increasing visibility in museum records. Newcombe often recorded details such as places of collection, names of sources and owners, how the objects were used and vocabulary relating to the objects (as he understood it) that are missing from the documentation for earlier collections. Just as Franz Boas depended largely on George Hunt of Fort Rupert for cultural objects and information, Newcombe had local First Nations sources of knowledge such as Charlie Nowell (Kwakwa̱ka̱'wakw), Henry Edenshaw (Haida)

FACING: Nuxalk mask from Bella Coola, *First Peoples* gallery.

and Atlieu family members (Nuu-chah-nulth). His travels and extensive personal networks throughout BC resulted in exceptional access to information and objects that is reflected in the collections he made for the provincial museum.

On his collecting trips, Newcombe made many photographs that are an informative aspect of the Newcombe collections in the Royal BC Museum and elsewhere. The images he took of poles and other cultural objects, houses and people, which are part of our audio-visual collections, provide context for the artifacts he collected and also reveal the extent to which photography had become an integral part of the collecting process.[9]

Newcombe continued collecting for international museums right up to his death in 1924, but the provincial museum's interest and funding had ended by 1914. His son William A. Newcombe (1900–1961) took over the collecting business after Charles died, and in 1928 became assistant curator of biology at the provincial museum on the basis of the work he had done with his father. But William's relationship with Curator Francis Kermode was strained, and he was dismissed in 1933.

After William died in 1961, the province purchased the Newcombe family's personal collection, including archival materials. Unfortunately, not all of the artifacts had specific documentation attached to them. The extensive "Newcombe Family Papers" (MS-1077) in our archives, however, are full of information in the form of correspondence, accounts, field notebooks, object lists and collection notes. One of our dedicated ethnology volunteers, Shelagh Graham, spent years combing the Newcombe papers for references to objects in the Royal BC Museum and other museums and made many connections. The challenge involved knowledge of Charles Newcombe's travels and correspondents, and deciphering his illegible handwriting. The findings enhance our understanding of the collection's context and sources.

Toward Authenticity (Mid 20th Century)

The BC Provincial Museum's active engagement with First Peoples dates from the early 1950s. Wilson Duff (1925–76) was hired as the anthropologist in 1950. A year later, Mungo Martin, Chief Na̱ka̱p̓a̱nka̱m (1881–1962), a Kwagu'ł artist from Tsax̱is (Fort Rupert, now part of Port Hardy on northern Vancouver Island), was hired to replicate and restore the deteriorating poles in Thunderbird Park. Martin and his family changed Thunderbird Park from an eccentric amalgamation of monumental carvings with no relationship to their original contexts to a site of active engagement with First Nations individuals. Duff, who was the museum's first trained curator of anthropology and worked closely with Martin on the Thunderbird Park redevelopment, changed the nature of institutional collecting when he arranged an exchange of replica Gitxsan poles for the originals, with permission contingent on the public acknowledgment of indigenous meanings and chiefly owners.

FACING: View of the *First Peoples* gallery showing, left to right, a Haida house post from hlragilda 'llnagaay (Skidegate), a Gitxsan house post from Gitanyow and a Haida house frontal pole from t'anuu 'llnagaay (Tanu).

First Nations cultures in BC are extremely diverse. There are 34 distinct linguistic groups in the province—more than any other region in the country—and within those groups are many different languages and dialects. Recognizing and reflecting this diversity means that old museum classifications are being overwritten with First Nations histories and intellectual concepts. Building on the Royal BC Museum's tradition of collaboration, our exhibitions and projects are now done in partnership with First Nations institutions and individuals.

ABOVE: Chief Nakap̓ankam, Mungo Martin, painting a Cannibal Bird mask in the carving studio, Thunderbird Park, 1953.

Collection from Mungo Martin, Chief Nakap̓ankam

Some of the poles that Charles Newcombe collected, along with other provincially owned monumental carvings, were installed in Thunderbird Park in 1942. Their arrangement combined carvings from different language groups and obscured any contextual information that Newcombe may have recorded in his notebooks and photographs. The carvings were placed in arbitrary relationships that had little or no connection with their cultural origins or living First Nations people. For example, Huu-ay-aht and Gusgimaxw house posts and a Haida frontal pole were all incorporated into a structure loosely based on a Haida six-beam house, and a Nuxalk house fontal pole stood in the middle of an Ahousaht painted ceremonial screen. When Mungo Martin arrived in Victoria in 1952, all this changed.

Assisted by members of his family, Martin carved replicas and new poles to replace the ones in Thunderbird Park that had deteriorated (the old poles were gradually removed to inside storage). To replace the ersatz house structure in Thunderbird Park, Martin built Wawadit̓ła, a smaller version of a famous house that once stood in Tsaxis. The house-front design was based on ones in Gwa'yasdams (on Gilford Island) and Tsadzis'nukwame' (New Vancouver on Harbledown Island) that Charles Newcombe photographed in 1900. In 1953 Martin inaugurated Wawadit̓ła with the first legal public potlatch held after the prohibition against potlatching was dropped from the Indian Act.

Martin carved Cannibal Bird masks (*hi'hamsiwe'*) and a four-headed Cannibal Bird mask (*mugums*) for use in the opening ceremonies in Wawadit̓ła, the first

Chief Na̱ḵap̓a̱nka̱m, Mungo Martin, and Mrs Helen Hunt present a copper to Elizabeth, the Queen Mother, in Windsor Great Park, 1958. The Queen's totem pole carved by Martin is in the background.

day of which "was for Indians only, so that Mungo Martin could perform his traditional ceremonies and display his masks and dances in a setting as authentic as possible [and was] a completely authentic and serious affair, not a show for outsiders."[10] When the museum purchased the Cannibal Bird masks in 1959, along with other objects owned by Martin, they came with a different order of interpretation than had previous collections. For example, the four-headed Cannibal Bird is also a *ługwe* (treasure) that the chief has a prerogative to show. The main bird, a type of Crooked-Beak called *galu'kwəmł,* is the form taken by the wife of Baxwbakwalanuxwsiwe' when she hunted food. The Ravens and the Huxwhukw on the mask are those worn by Baxwbakwalanuxwsiwe' "when he flies to get food." Martin carved the masks while on staff and the masks are in the museum's collection, but their status as museum objects does not erase the ongoing connection with their First Nations owners. The four-headed Cannibal Bird mask was the hereditary cultural property of Martin's grandson, Chief Oast̓a̱ka̱laga̱lis 'Walas 'Na̱mugwis, Peter Knox, of Fort Rupert. The family owns another version of this important mask that Chief Knox's son, 'Maxwa̱'yalisdzi, David Knox, carved for use in their potlatches. Chief Peter Knox passed away in 2014 and the cultural ownership of the mask will be passed to the next generation.

Through his work at the BC Provincial Museum, Martin demonstrated connections between museum objects and intangible heritage. He recorded songs and oral histories with the museum's anthropologist, Wilson Duff. Martin and his family developed personal relationships with museum staff and were sources of information and connections to Kwakwa̱ka̱'wakw and other First Nations communities. They brought First Nations individuals into the museum and demonstrated links between them and the cultural objects that had come into the collection years before. They also engaged the public who were able to see and talk to them while they worked in the carving shed at Thunderbird Park. For many residents and tourists, these interactions were probably their first personal encounters with First Nations people. A book about

Watercolour painting on paper of
Bird and Whale by Chief Na̲ka̲p̓a̲nka̲m,
Mungo Martin, 1960.

Martin describes him as a "man of two cultures."[11] At the Provincial Museum his presence began to form a bridge between First Nations and non-aboriginal people. Martin's painted curtain (*mawił*) that is now in the museum's collection illustrates his program that made First Nations culture visible in an urban setting. The huge curtain was hung in Kwakwa̱ka̱'wakw big houses during important potlatches, but it also formed the centre piece of a float that Martin and his family entered in the 1955 Victoria Day parade. For this event, the same design was painted on the back of the curtain so that it could be seen by people on both sides of the parade route. Both the potlatches and the parade were recorded in photographs, an increasingly important factor in museum documentation.

Martin was initially seen by the museum as an educational resource for the public, a cultural authority and a sort of living specimen of a vanishing carving tradition, but within two years of his arrival in Victoria, he and his family took ownership of a major part of Thunderbird Park, dominated the anthropology department and permanently transformed the museum's thinking about Aboriginal culture in contemporary BC.[12]

Collection from Wilson Duff

Wilson Duff was the museum's first formally trained anthropologist, with a BA in anthropology from the University of British Columbia and a MA from the University of Washington. Upon his arrival in 1950, Duff assumed responsibility for the construction of Wawadiťła and the totem pole carving program in Thunderbird Park. There he received a different kind of training in First Nations cultures. One of the projects he took on during his tenure created a radically new understanding of the connections between contemporary First Nations people and museum objects, demonstrated indigenous meanings inherent in cultural objects and articulated the ethical and educational responsibilities of museums.

In 1958 Wilson Duff, representing the BC Provincial Museum, and Michael Kew of the University of British Columbia, representing the Totem Pole Preservation Committee, went to Kitwancool (Gitanyow) to negotiate the removal of a small number of poles for preservation at the museum.[13] The chiefs and people of Gitanyow accepted the committee's proposal to make replica poles and erect them at Gitanyow in place of the originals, but only on condition that "their histories, territories and laws were to be written down, published and made available to the University for teaching purposes."[14] A formal contract was drawn up and signed. The museum recorded the stories of the poles that were dictated by Gitanyow chiefs and published them as *Histories, Territories and Laws of the Kitwancool* in 1959. With this contract, the museum entered into a relationship involving long-term obligations, including ensuring that the book was always available, encouraging its use in university courses so that generations of students would learn about Gitanyow,

FACING: A masterpiece of Haida carving: argillite chest attributed to da.a xiigang, Charles Edenshaw (1839–1920). A detail view of the same chest is on pages 2–3.

and informing "the officials of the University that the people of Kitwancool would welcome suggestions for the improvement of their legal position and welfare." This contract, published in full in the book, was the first formal collaboration between a museum and a Northwest Coast First Nation. It was "a remarkable agreement and publication by a government that only in 1990 agreed to negotiate the land issue in BC [that established] a very different kind of relationship with Native Peoples... recognizing traditional ownership and authority."[15]

This agreement brought cultural objects into the museum's collection in a new way, setting the benchmark for subsequent acquisitions, and with unprecedented documentation that brought new understandings of the complex historical and legal meanings inherent in all such objects. The Gitanyow poles are the Wolf house (*wilp*) pole of Gaa-quk-dik-giat, the Wolf house pole of Skim-sim and Will-a-daugh, and the Frog house pole of Chief Gwen-nu, named Nee-gamks. The histories they tell include how the Wolf and Frog houses (*huwilp*) came to occupy their current territories and the extent of those territories. As Duff acknowledged in his introduction to the narratives set down in *Histories, Territories and Laws of the Kitwancool*, these accounts support the Gitanyow's claims to ownership of their traditional lands: "The totem poles stand as visible symbols of these histories (which were related whenever a pole was erected), and in a sense are considered as legal deeds to the territories concerned.... The territorial claims and concepts of ownership are stated in explicit terms in the later sections of the book."[16]

The Gitanyow agreement expressed what poles mean and do, and illustrated the relevance of historical meanings to contemporary social and political issues. Early collectors like Deans saw poles as artifacts that could be removed physically and conceptually from their places of origin. *Histories, Territories and Laws of the Kitwancool* forced an understanding that the original poles might be removed only with the formal consent of their chiefly owners and, wherever they are physically located, the meanings embodied by the poles remain permanently connected to those chiefs and their places of origin, and have ongoing philosophical and legal ramifications.

New Understandings of Collections
(Mid to Late 20th Century)

The carving program in Thunderbird Park that was initiated by Mungo Martin and overseen by Wilson Duff until his departure for the University of British Columbia in 1965 played a role in the renewal of Northwest Coast art traditions in the mid 20th century, and also contributed to the florescence of contemporary potlatching. Carving-program artists made new versions of masks and other regalia in the museum's collection that were loaned out for use in ceremonies, thus helping to support the bringing out of hereditary

rights and privileges that had not been shown publically throughout the period of the potlatch ban. (The potlatch, other ceremonies and large gatherings were illegal under the Indian Act between 1884 and 1951.) With the advent of modern treaties and legal decisions confirming First Nations rights to self-determination and title to traditional territories, the idea of sharing the museum's collections now includes physical permanent transfers in addition to loans and "virtual repatriation" through public databases.

The Carving Program and the Potlatch Collection

Mungo Martin brought his family to Victoria when he came to work at the museum. He was assisted in Thunderbird Park by his son, David Martin (who died in a fishing accident in 1959), by Henry Hunt (1923–85), who was married to Martin's adopted daughter, Helen, and by Henry's son Tony Hunt (1942–). The carving program that began in 1952 continued for many years, although funding was always precarious. Henry Hunt became chief carver after Martin's death. He and Tony both resigned in the mid 1970s, and Henry's younger son Richard (1951–) became head carver. Richard was followed by Tim Paul (1950–), a Nuu-chah-nulth artist. A number of carvers worked at various times in the program, many of whom went on to distinguished art careers. After 1986 the carving program became a partnership with the Victoria Native Friendship Centre. The program ceased in 2008 when the carving studio building, which was the third carving studio on the site, was found to be no longer structurally sound and had to be pulled down.

The potlatch collection was a significant outcome of the carving program and a new kind of collaboration with First Nations individuals: carvers working in Thunderbird Park made versions of museum objects that were loaned for use in ceremonies to First Nations people who held the hereditary rights to use them. The carvings helped to further the development of First Nations art forms and played a role in the continuation of potlatches and ceremonies. The museum's collection of modern objects benefited. Museum staff learned about First Nations cultural practices and protocols, and developed ongoing relationships with potlatching families (who were mostly Kwakwaka'wakw).

As Ira Jacknis has pointed out, the carving program played an important role in the formation of the museum's collections, too.[17] Wilson Duff's acquisition of the Gitanyow poles was made possible by exchanging them for replica poles carved in Victoria, primarily by Henry Hunt. When Peter Macnair (1940–) became curator of ethnology in 1965, the strategy of exchange continued and broadened to allow objects to go back and forth between the museum and First Nations communities. An exchange may have been part of an acquisition as it was in the purchase of an old frontlet from Alice Smith in 1973. As part of the transaction, Smith was given a new version of the frontlet carved by Richard Hunt, which eventually came back to the museum with the purchase of her estate.[18]

Usually, though, First Nations families could borrow new versions of their regalia for ceremonial use. In the art market, the monetary value of a mask or other piece of regalia increased if it had been used in an authentic ritual. In the museum context, the added value was in terms of accurate documentation, new insights about use and ownership, personalizing the institution and, not least, fulfilling the museum's responsibility to make collections accessible as appropriate. A ledger listing the potlatches and how the objects were used in them was maintained and, since Macnair or other staff accompanied the objects to the communities, photographs and notes added to the documentation of the object.

The nature of museum documentation had changed radically, along with ideas about the relationships between the museum and the communities the objects had come from. The salvage paradigm of the late 19th century that saw sources of artifacts as anonymous cultural ciphers had a century later been replaced by an ethnical requirement to maintain and express links between museum objects and specific individuals or First Nations. Peter Macnair held his position as curator of ethnology for 31 years, retiring in 1996. During his tenure, he brought First Nations communities into the museum and insisted that the museum live up to its commitments as a custodian of cultural objects from those communities. The museum's role went from watcher to participant, from established cultural authority to student. The value of connecting collections with living communities that Macnair articulated and demonstrated through his work remains a core value of the Royal BC Museum. We are still able to loan material for First Nations ceremonial use from time to time, but this happens less frequently because people now have their own regalia.

Treaties

The value of objects going back and forth between the museum and their places of origin continues to be recognized. Now, though, an increasing acknowledgement of First Nations rights to hereditary territories and cultural interpretation goes beyond temporary loans for specific purposes to actual not just symbolic repatriation.

As the provincial collection, the Royal BC Museum is the only museum in the province that is part of the treaty negotiation process. We provide artifact inventories, documentation, collections visits, advice on policy and information as required to the Ministry of Aboriginal Relations and Reconciliation's negotiators. Treaty negotiations impact museum policy and practice, and also affect how the collection and its documentation are conceptualized.

Under the terms of the Nisg̲a'a Final Agreement of 2000, which was the first modern treaty in BC, the Royal BC Museum transferred 155 objects and all legal title to them to the Nisg̲a'a Nation. The Nisg̲a'a built a beautiful new museum at Lax̲g̲alts'ap (formerly Greenville) in the Nass Valley to house these objects,

FACING: *Salish Loom*, an artwork by Musqueam artist Debra Sparrow, commissioned for the *Our Living Languages* exhibition.

Changing concepts and engagements with First Nations have been reflected in exhibitions, most recently, *Our Living Languages—First Peoples Voices in British Columbia*, a formal partnership with the First Peoples' Cultural Council that inserts new meanings and Indigenous values into the museum's galleries.

q
x
m̓
n̓

Storytellers and Language Keepers by Haida artist Jaalen Edenshaw, commissioned for *Our Living Languages.*

along with others transferred by the Canadian Museum of History. The objects were delivered to Laxgalts'ap in September 2010, and the Nisga'a museum, called Hli Goothl Wilp-Adokshl Nisga'a (The Heart of Nisga'a House Crests), opened with great ceremony on May 11, 2011, the anniversary of the ratification of the Nisga'a Treaty.

The Nisga'a Final Agreement predates today's formal treaty negotiation process, but the provisions with regard to artifacts have proved to be a template of sorts for subsequent treaty language to date. One of the things that treaty negotiations have highlighted is the inadequacy of the 19th-century museum classifications based on broad language classifications: Athapaskan, which designated all Dene First Nations; Tsimshian, which encompassed Coast Tsimshian, Gitxsan and Nisga'a; Kwakiutl, which at one time included Kwakwaka'wakw, Heiltsuk, Haisla and Wuikinuxv; and many other general terms. These classifications are not very useful from our contemporary perspective, especially for First Nations looking for cultural objects from their specific territories. Museum classifications and terminology need to be more precise about origin and source, but, as we have seen, these details were not always recorded by collectors.

Treaties create new classifications, too. For example, five Nuu-chah-nulth nations—Che:k'tles7et'h', Ka:'yu:'k't'h', Ucluelet, Huu-ay-aht, Toquaht and Uchucklesaht—ratified the Maa-nulth Final Agreement in 2011, and the Royal BC Museum will transfer cultural objects to each of these nations upon request. The Maa-nulth nations are not contiguous and have never been a single entity, but the name Maa-nulth is now a Nuu-chah-nulth division in the museum's catalogue records. Thus, the treaty emphasizes the unstable nature of museum classification. (The name, Nuu-chah-nulth, itself is a modern designation for the language group formerly known as Nootka and later, for a brief time, called Westcoast.) Museums have long recognized that First Nations and museological classifications are often at odds with one another. Now we have another layer of labelling and sorting within a structure of treaty negotiations. Re-examination and re-conceptualization of the catalogue is required, yet maintaining the integrity and accuracy of the original collection records and subsequent additions and interpretations remains critical.[19]

The museum's Nuu-chah-nulth collections for transfer are mainly from Charles Newcombe, as were the objects transferred to the Nisga'a Nation. For this museum, treaties mean the division of the Newcombe collection and, if other First Nations ratify treaties, of other significant single-collector groups of objects. Museums are accustomed to seeing these collections as units and historical structures that carry many meanings: interactions, cultural loss, economic realities, unequal power relationships, enforcement of non-aboriginal values by church and state, movements and associations of peoples, languages, terminology,

FACING: Kwakwa̱ka̱'wakw artist Francis Dick with her work *Interactive Language Light Pillar,* commissioned for *Our Living Languages.*

style and dates, and so on. The division of a collection breaks up the group of objects, and may, over time, break up the documentation and historical links of this kind of knowledge and thinking about objects. But while collections like Newcombe's are broken up physically by treaties, they are not alienated. The transferred Nisg̱a'a objects can now be seen in their own territory at the Nisg̱a'a museum. Online databases make it possible to reconstitute collections in a different form and we gain new understandings and new kinds of information about the collections and their context.

People and Partnerships

(Late 20th Century to the Present)

First Nations cultures in BC are extremely diverse. There are 34 distinct linguistic groups in the province—more than any other region in the country—and within those groups are many different languages and dialects. Recognizing and reflecting this diversity means that old museum classifications are being overwritten with First Nations histories and intellectual concepts. Building on the Royal BC Museum's tradition of collaboration, our exhibitions and projects are now done in partnership with First Nations institutions and individuals.

Changing concepts and engagements with First Nations, such as those outlined above, have altered our methods of collecting and of documenting our collections. These changes have been reflected in exhibitions, publications and other projects over time in partnership with First Nations, including the Hesquiaht Project (began 1970), the *First Peoples* gallery (opened 1977), *The Legacy* exhibition and book (1980), *HuupuKʷanum-Tupaat: Out of the Mist, Treasures of the Nuu-chah-nulth Chiefs* exhibition and book (1999), *Nisg̱a'a—People of the Nass River* exhibition (2002), *'Nłuut'iksa Łagigyedm Ts'msyeen: Treasures of the Tsimshian from the Dundas Collection* exhibition (2007) and, most recently, *Our Living Languages—First Peoples Voices in British Columbia* exhibition (2014), a formal partnership with the First Peoples' Cultural Council that inserts new meanings and indigenous values into the Royal BC Museum's galleries.

The history of the Royal BC Museum's collections and their documentation reflects changing attitudes and often difficult negotiations between First Nations and settler populations. Our museum has been, and continues to be, a place where these changes are both mirrored and initiated. Our issues are local, but they pertain to other colonial societies coming to terms with past discriminatory policies and working toward reconciliation and new relationships with once-marginalized original populations.

The Royal BC Museum has learned from the patient, and often not so patient, demands by First Nations for inclusion in the museum and authority over the interpretation of the objects from their ancestors and communities. It is an ongoing process that will result in new and different classifications and forms of documentation in the future.

RICHARD J. HEBDA

LIVING LANDSCAPES

SUPER NATURAL BRITISH COLUMBIA

BRITISH COLUMBIA IS big, wild and different from any other place on Earth. Here, nature dominates our landscapes. There are lots of people, but unlike many places on our planet, human communities are highly concentrated, clustered near the border with the United States and on a few major rivers, lakes and harbours. The plants, fungi and animals still live mostly as they have for thousands of years. This natural legacy has been explored, documented and displayed by the Royal BC Museum for nearly 130 years, drawing millions of visitors from around the world. Yet there remains much to be discovered.

Our understanding of British Columbia's natural inheritance is rooted in the provincial museum's collections, containing millions of objects gathered, documented, described and studied by our experts and many others around the world. The museum's natural history collections have played an especially

FACING: A Cougar in the dry coastal forest of southeast Vancouver Island, part of the forest diorama in the *Natural History* gallery. The Elk on the previous spread are part of the same diorama.

key role in understanding the diversity of life in British Columbia and in the northern hemisphere. They include objects that span the size spectrum of life on Earth, from microscopic flies to the skeletons of whales. Our 600,000 insect specimens provide the basis for anyone, be they expert or member of the public, to identify and name what they find in nature. We sometimes forget the importance of identification. Without knowing what a creature is we cannot manage it, we cannot talk about it, we cannot really appreciate its role in our lives, and we cannot satisfy our curiosity to understand what it represents.

The museum's collections link us not only to British Columbia's seascapes and landscapes, they also connect us to the rest of Earth's natural world and to global human communities. Our fossils track the history of life on Earth through some of its most crucial stages, such as the evolution of hard body parts revealed in the world-famous Burgess Shale. They provide insight fundamental to understanding the origin of major life groupings, species and biomes (such as the tundra). Our plant collections reveal the ice-age connections of North America to Asia and Europe. They demonstrate how past and modern climates have shaped and continue to shape the patterns of life on Earth today. Our vertebrate collections document some of the most iconic creatures on the planet, such as the Grizzly Bear (*Ursus arctos*). On the other hand, they provide the raw material for recent revelations that there are more shrew species than we had once thought. Collections of invertebrates from our cold ocean waters have led to the discovery of new species, and doubtless hold many discoveries yet to come from the watery realm. And the dizzying array of insects is almost impossible to comprehend, with new creatures being discovered at a remarkable rate.

Obviously there is scientific power and the beauty of order in the size and comprehensiveness of large collections, but their real essence lies in the individual specimens and objects. Each specimen represents a unique set of circumstances and offers unique stories and insights. By observing many specimens, we develop a general model or concept and begin to understand the species. Yet, at the same time, we also discover the range of variation in a species, and appreciate that each individual has had its own remarkable experiences.

Let's explore British Columbia and its global connections and importance by looking at its vast, diverse and unique natural legacy. The story that follows is firmly rooted in my three and a half decades at the Royal BC Museum and thousands of hours exploring and collecting in our province. It rests on my shared experiences with colleagues past and present. It is especially informed by the exceptional curators and collection managers at our institution today. To their work now and in the future we owe much debt. We can only imagine what they will discover next.

Deep Time

Our voyage begins with the physical landscape itself. The form and structure of the land provide the foundation for all life. The roots of our place run deep, following diverse pathways to distinctive landforms and ecosystems. We cannot collect landscapes, of course, but we can collect representations of them, in the form of field notes, sketches, photographs, written impressions—these are as much part of the natural history collections as biological and geological specimens.

For its size, British Columbia is one of the most geologically rich places on Earth. Our rocks span at least two billion years and include one of the most complete records of ancient life on the globe.

The province is constructed, as consequence of continental drift, of more major yet different fragments of crust than almost anywhere else of similar size on the planet. Starting with the venerable and persistent North American continental core in the east, at least seven major crustal masses known as terranes have been sutured to its western edge. These include the uplifted depths of two oceans. The rocks representing this incredible time (nearly half the history of the Earth) would collectively stack up hundreds of kilometres thick. And those rocks represent just about every kind of geological process and deposit known on the globe.

Shales from the blackest depths of the deepest Triassic seas can be found squeezed up into alpine heights in the northern Rocky Mountains. Limestones and reefs from warm ancient Paleozoic waters abound throughout the Rockies, too. Rich and diverse shoreline sandstones and mudstones from the Cretaceous Period (145 to 65 million years ago) drape over the ancient geologic basement of east Vancouver Island and the Gulf Islands. Ancient swamp forests, long ago turned to coal in southeastern BC, now fuel the furnaces of Asia. The shales and sandstones associated with them also preserve fascinating footprints of dinosaurs. Thick volcanic flows underlie the heart of the province between coastal and eastern mountain masses, holding petrified forests and yielding colourful agates. The lava cliffs provide unique habitats for Western Rattlesnakes and Black Widow spiders.

British Columbia even hosts several volcanic monsters active not so long ago, such as Mount Edziza in the northwest, from which glassy black obsidian provided the raw material for the cutting tools of our first inhabitants. Gigantic granite intrusions have forced their way into the roots of the crust throughout geological time, concentrating metals such as gold and copper, and fuelling a dynamic mining industry. A few exceptional natural examples of these metals have made their way into our collections.

Landforms of Every Shape and Size

Rocks don't just form. They age, they crumble, they get crushed and transformed by internal and external processes. These processes lead to a wide array of landforms that are central to the diversity and distribution of British Columbia's species and ecosystems.

A fossil trilobite (*Ogygopsis klotzii*) typical of the discoveries made during the building of the Canadian Pacific Railroad—this one was found near Field, British Columbia.

Unstable rock fields and windswept bedrock provide niches for plants and animals to survive in alpine regions. Steep mountain cliffs and slopes face different exposures from the shadowy cold north to the bright hot south, leading to enormous habitat variation over short distances. Deep, rich soils on lower slopes sustain some of the most productive forests on Earth. Next to them, valley-bottom flood plains and rivers support great populations of fishes. During the last ice age, while much of the province lay buried beneath glaciers, the crumbling edifices of some coastal mountains, as on Haida Gwaii, sustained unique plant species.

The Sweep of Ancient Life

Our museum's fossil collections reveal the meanderings of various pieces of the Earth's crust jostled over hundreds of millions of years by continental drift. They track the history of life from ancient oceans to recent struggles to survive frigid glacial climates. And they illustrate the magnificent designs of form and function for making a living from lightless abysses to subtropical forests. British Columbia fossils present a record of life as diverse and complex as anywhere on Earth.

Our story in British Columbia begins with soft-bodied creatures that left filmy traces in rocks 550 million years old near Mount Robson. We do not know what these organisms were—jellyfish, worms, algae? Whatever their identity, they led to one of the great explosions of life, preserved at what some biologists call the most important fossil site on Earth: the Burgess Shale in Yoho National Park (part of a UNESCO World Heritage site). The Burgess Shale holds exquisitely preserved organisms, some with shells and some without, that belonged to a complex marine ecosystem. Some, like the lace crab (*Marrella*), look vaguely familiar, while others have no obvious modern descendants. Among them is the first giant predator, *Anomalocharis*, a metre long with big eyes and fearsome mouth parts. In nearby beds swam a great variety of stunningly beautiful trilobites, such as *Ogygopsis klotzii*, that may have been the favourite meal of *Anomalocharis*.

British Columbia is big, wild and different from any other place on Earth. Here, nature dominates our landscapes. There are lots of people, but human communities are highly concentrated, clustered near the border with the United States and on a few major rivers, lakes and harbours. The plants, fungi and animals still live mostly as they have for thousands of years.

RICHARD HEBDA

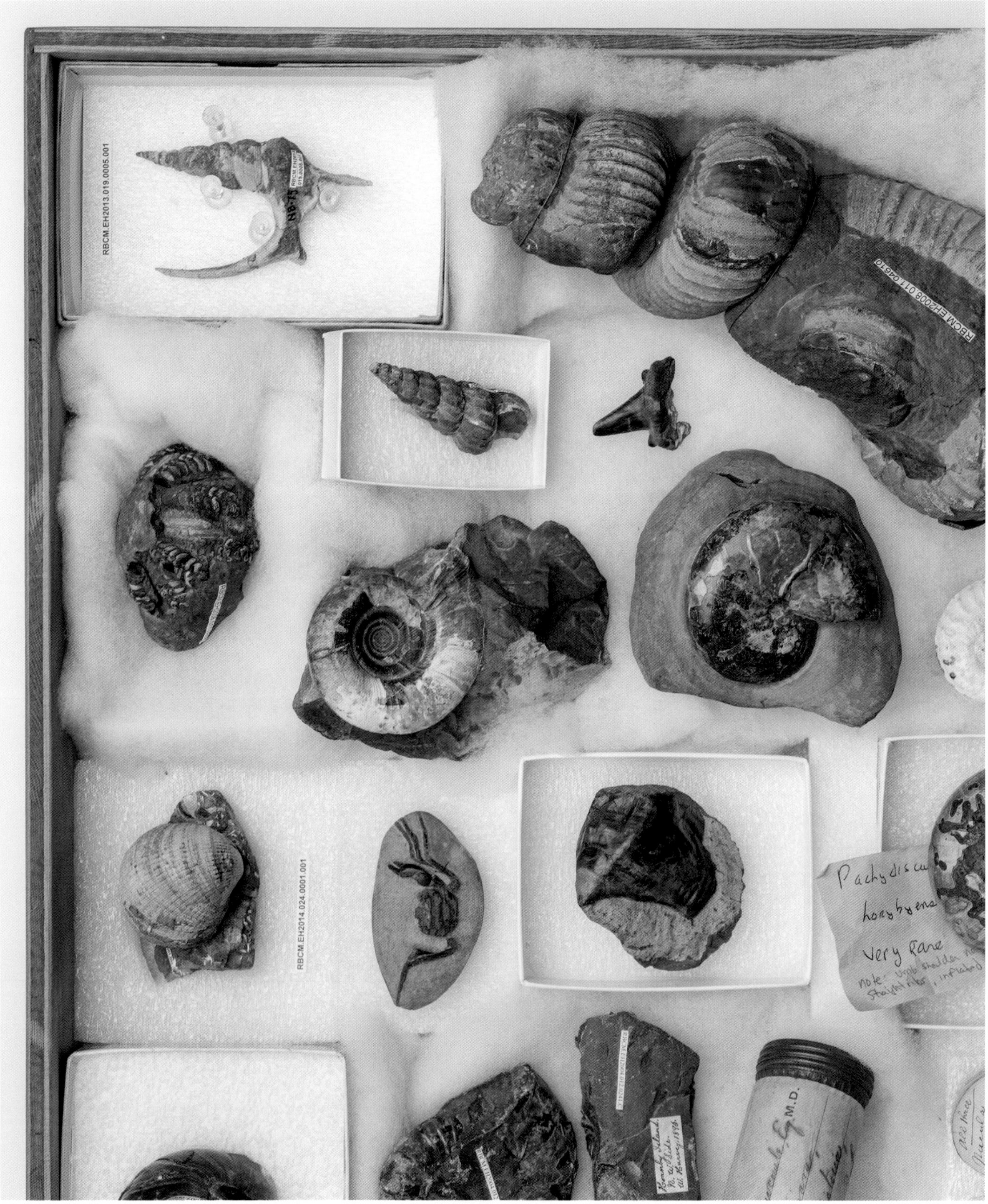
RBCM.EH2013.019.0005.001
RBCM.EH2014.024.0001.001
Very Rare
M.D.

FACING: Fossils, 75-80 million years old, of the Cretaceous Period, from eastern Vancouver Island and Gulf Islands. Visible are clams, snails, crabs, ammonites and even the tooth of a shark.

The diversification of marine life during the Paleozoic is also well displayed in many sites in the Rocky Mountains and on Vancouver Island, but the fossil bounty of this province is best illustrated by our Mesozoic deposits ranging from 251 million to 65 million years in age. Rocks from alpine heights near Wapiti Lake in east-central BC have produced spectacular specimens of large coelacanths. These fish, known as "living fossils," are still with us today, but were first known as fossils. Our specimens are complete individuals preserved on massive slabs of rock plucked by helicopter from isolated mountain slopes. They were only one group among many other types of fish, also preserved in detail at the site.

British Columbia has its dinosaurs, too. Many came to light in the vicinity of Tumbler Ridge and are now on display at the local museum and research centre. But recent discoveries of tracks and bones in the isolated wild country of north-central BC point to a new unexplored dinosaur region waiting for future paleontologists.

The sandstone and shale of Vancouver Island and the Gulf Islands hold one of the best records of life of the Upper Cretaceous Period (100 to 65 million years ago) on the planet. Our cabinets and shelves hold as many as 35,000 specimens, many of them donated by highly skilled amateur collectors. The diversity of form of the now-extinct ammonites is a feast for the eyes—picture a giant snail with a squid's head sticking out of the shell. These molluscan predators ruled the Mesozoic seas. Our fossil collection includes ammonites with flat, spiralled shells that reach up to two metres across, others with fat, tire-like shells, and strange open-coiled and paper-clip-shaped heteromorphs that may have simply floated about in the seaweeds lurking to nab prey. These ammonites had intricately complex walls separating gas chambers in the shell to help them stay buoyant in the ocean depths.

Mesozoic land ecosystems are represented by massive coal deposits that underpin the province's economy. Today our coal comes from beds in the eastern part of the province, but at one time, Vancouver Island coal was a major source for the world and helped to build local wealth. Fantastic fossil leaf beds, including giant palms, are associated with these coals. The palms indicate that parts of Vancouver Island once had a subtropical climate. The Upper Cretaceous was among the warmest intervals in the Earth's history with average temperatures up to 10°C warmer than today and a high amount of carbon dioxide in the atmosphere.

Volcanoes and lava flows have dominated the Cenozoic Era for the last 65 million years. Yet warm lakes occurred widely and their sediments preserved a most magnificent record of plant and animal life.

Fine volcanic ash in particular helped preserve the most delicate features of fossil specimens, such as the hairs of insects at the Eocene Epoch McAbee Heritage Fossil Beds near Cache Creek, which are 53 million years old. Many previously undiscovered insect species are being revealed from these deposits—the number will eventually reach more than 300—as well as fishes, birds and flowers. The site may become the most scientifically important of its age on the globe.

It's hard to say whether ice-age mammoths have made our museum famous or our museum has made them even more famous. Either way, British Columbia has a rich ice-age fauna, from mammoths to short-faced bears, demonstrating that our climates and landscapes were very different just a few thousand years ago. The remains of these now-extinct beasts teach us that when climate changes everything changes, and they serve as an unsettling reminder that the living landscapes of the near-future will not be the same as those familiar to us today.

Of Ecosystems and Plants

British Columbia's ecological canvas is stunningly complex, not just because of the province's size, but because of the underlying landforms and climatic diversity. So diverse is BC's ecology that scientists have defined 16 distinct *biogeoclimatic* zones. Two of these, the Sub-boreal Spruce and Sub-boreal Pine-spruce biogeoclimatic zones of central BC, are found nowhere else in the world. And the global range of four other zones occur mostly in our province. Our stands of the Coastal Western Hemlock zone, the iconic brooding conifer forests of Emily Carr paintings, constitute the largest area of original temperate rainforest left in the world. These stands support some of the largest trees on Earth. The geographical pattern of the zones is remarkable too. In southern BC one can cross 6 of the 16 zones in a latitudinal distance of just seven kilometres, from hot, dry bunchgrass lands to frigid alpine tundra.

This complex ecological palette creates the habitats for more vascular plant species than anywhere else in Canada. These plants form the living natural framework of British Columbia. They capture energy from the sun and turn it into food for almost all other organisms. For humans they have provided food, medicines and building materials for millennia, and economic opportunity and spiritual inspiration for residents and visitors.

The remarkable diversity of BC's plants is represented by 215,000 specimens in the Royal BC Museum's herbarium. Botany Curator Ken Marr calls this collection a "dried plant library," because it contains thoroughly documented real examples of nearly every vascular plant species found in the province, from gigantic Sitka Spruces (*Picea sitchensis*) to minute duckweeds (*Lemna* species). Our specimens include pioneering collections of John Macoun, a naturalist with the Geological Survey of Canada in the 1890s, and examples of long-gone populations eliminated by urban and agricultural expansion. The specimens also provide testimony of the remarkable knowledge of First Nations elders, such as Soapberry

Erica Wheeler, collection manager of the herbarium, preparing typical specimens of pressed plants.

Showy Milkweed (*Asclepias speciosa*), a native plant from the southern interior of British Columbia

(*Shepherdia canadensis*) collected by ethnobotanists as they learned from Ulkatcho Carrier elders in the west Chilcotin region. Our collections grow as new species come to our shores and farmlands and challenge the future of those long-established in this unique corner of the world. They also grow as botanists from or associated with this museum visit isolated corners of the province never before explored.

One of the most important functions of biological collections, whether they contain marine worms or plants, is to help advance the understanding of life around the world. Our museum has sent tens of thousands of specimens to international experts who develop up-to-date descriptions and classifications of the diversity of life. Our own curators use the collection for the same purpose. In 2007 Ken Marr and I contributed a treatment of North American reedgrasses (*Calamagrostis* species) to the first modern comprehensive account of all plants on the continent.

There remain large areas of the province for which the plant species are nearly unknown, because these hinterlands are difficult to get to. Until recently almost no collecting had been done in the wild and rugged northern parts of British Columbia, particularly the high mountains, one of the greatest alpine regions of the world. Since 2002 we have visited more than 100 remote peaks and plateaus. Fifteen thousand specimens have been collected so far and among them a fascinating plant not previously known to occur within the borders of BC: Icegrass (*Phippsia algida*) grows at frigid alpine heights and also occurs in Alaska, northern Canada, Wyoming and Colorado, but nowhere in between, despite there being much suitable habitat. At least 11 other species of tundra plants in western North America have a similar distribution. This species and its broken distribution range suggest that cold climates and tundra habitats were once widespread, even at low elevations, allowing it to spread to cold high mountains far from the northern tundra. Geographic patterns such as these raise questions about the extent, timing and intensity of global ice ages.

In collaboration with international colleagues, we are also studying the DNA of our northern collections and those from around the pole and mid latitude mountains, such as the Altai of southern Siberia, to probe the origin of our native flora, fauna and ecosystems.

Analyses of Mountain Sorrel (*Oxyria digyna*) DNA indicate that some individuals now living in BC are descendants of plants that migrated into the province from the north and south following the last ice ages. Surprisingly though, it appears that the ancestors of some Mountain Sorrel plants have been in BC for perhaps hundreds of thousands of years, surviving in ice-free refuges. It may even be that this widespread northern-hemisphere species arose in British Columbia before the last ice age began.

Insects and Arachnids

Bugs can be beautiful (as are butterflies and dragonflies), painful (certain wasps) and vital to our economy (pests and pollinators). They are certainly numerous and diverse; insects and arachnids (including spiders) make up more than 80 per cent of the world's animal species. Although they are of enormous interest and ecological importance, our knowledge of these two groups globally and in British Columbia remains limited. Nevertheless, the museum's sizeable and varied collections play a major role in our understanding of these numerically dominant organisms. In particular, our collections have helped us understand where rare and endangered species occur, and how they fit into exceptional ecosystems such as the province's nationally unique grasslands.

Rob Cannings (as a curator and now emeritus curator in entomology here) has played a central role in relating the fascinating stories of two major insect groups, dragonflies and robber flies. In so doing, he has highlighted the importance of BC as conduit between North America and Asia, and has identified biodiversity hot spots. BC is home to many stunningly beautiful and fascinating dragonfly species. Among them, the endangered Olive Clubtail (*Stylurus olivaceus*) illustrates the importance of comprehensive field collecting and of knowing where populations of rare species occur. It inhabits only three streams in BC (and in Canada), all with warm muddy bottoms and sandy banks in the nationally rare grasslands of the Okanagan.

Though not as stylish as dragonflies, robber flies have been a focus of our major international studies. *Efferia okanagana* (yet to receive a common name) was first discovered in the Okanagan desert and has been found nowhere else in the world. Its occurrence demonstrates that BC is home to unique creatures and suggests that further studies in the province are likely to reveal many more new species. Field collections by Rob Cannings and other museum staff and colleagues in wild sites across BC, such as the Ilgachuz Mountains of the Chilcotin, helped revolutionize our understanding of robber flies. For example, Cannings recognized for the first time that the Variable Robber Fly (*Rhadiurgus variabilis*), first named in Europe, was identical to a species later named in North America. We now know that this species ranges around the northern hemisphere, connecting our Canadian populations to those in Siberia and as far away as Scotland.

The museum's natural history collections have played an especially key role in understanding the diversity of life in British Columbia and in the northern hemisphere. They include objects that span the size spectrum of life on Earth, from microscopic flies to the skeletons of whales. They link us not only to British Columbia's seascapes and landscapes, they also connect us to the rest of Earth's natural world and to global human communities.

RICHARD HEBDA

Our wonderful butterflies reinforce hemispheric connections too. The magnificent Oregon Swallowtail (*Papilio machaon*) occurs as a subspecies (*P.m. oregonia*) in our southern grasslands and another subspecies in the Peace River district (*P.m. pikei*). The species re-appears in another form (*P.m. aliaska*) in the grasslands of Alaska, Yukon and extreme northern BC. It is closely related to various subspecies that range across northern Asia to Europe, where the butterfly is known as the Common Swallowtail. Its distribution pattern raises questions about the history of grasslands in western North America, and how and when they may have been connected to each other in the Americas and to Asia across the Bering Sea. Like the research into alpine plants, studies of this butterfly lead to questions about the extent and character of glacial ice sheets and how insects came to occupy the places and habitats they do today.

You may be surprised that we know of about 450 bee species living in BC and we expect to discover up to 100 more. The total amounts to more than half of the species in Canada. Recent museum collecting has focused on understanding bee distribution better and assessing how they are faring. In addition to the European Honey Bee (*Apis mellifera*) brought here for honey and pollination, bumble bees are another familiar group. Some of these are in serious decline—the Western Bumble Bee (*Bombus occidentalis*) is now considered a threatened species. The value of solitary bees such as the Orchard or Blue Mason bee (*Osmia lignaria*) is only now beginning to be appreciated. Understanding bee populations is vital to a sustainable food supply.

Though not insects, spiders have become a central focus of the work in entomology at the museum. They are one of the most diverse groups of animals on the planet—scientists estimate that only about half of the species have been discovered and described so far. British Columbia hosts some pretty famous spider characters, including the venomous-to-humans Black Widow (*Latrodectus hesperus*). Common to hot dry settings of the southern interior, Black Widows also inhabit dry sites on Vancouver Island. New spider species are being found everywhere in the province, from the deep mosses of coastal forests to windswept mountaintops. Museum entomologist Claudia Copley and several expert volunteers are turning over thousands of rocks, especially at high elevations, and collecting tiny spider species that have been overlooked. Several new species wait in the collections to be described shortly. They have just described an extremely speedy spider, *Apostenus ducati*, as a result of this work.

Treasures from the Sea

British Columbia's enormously long coastline and complex underwater topography offer a variety of environments, from estuaries to fjord troughs to abyssal plains. Our coastal waters have sustained people for thousands of years and fostered historic communities along its shores. The ocean is home to stunningly beautiful

Bubblegum Coral (*Paragorgia arborea*), an exquisite species found in the cold, deep waters of British Columbia's fjords.

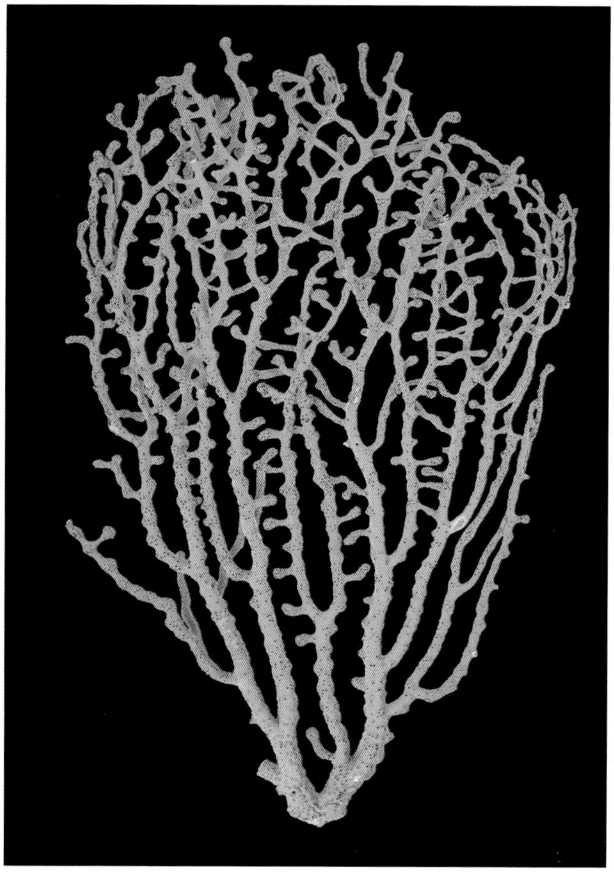

organisms that enrich our planetary biological diversity, and it regularly yields new species for us to cherish and understand. As Curator of Invertebrates Melissa Frey puts it, BC's ocean waters connect us to the world.

Our invertebrate collection contains marine animals such as worms, clams and sponges. The museum has been collecting marine invertebrates for more than a century—we now have at least 65,000 lots, some consisting of single species and some with many individuals of many species. Even so, Frey estimates that we know about only half of possibly 10,000 invertebrate species that live here.

Some of our superstar invertebrates are familiar, such as the world's largest octopus, *Enteroctopus dofleini*, the Giant Pacific Octopus. Other record holders for size include the Gumboot Chiton (*Cryptochiton stelleri*), the Giant Acorn Barnacle (*Balanus nubilus*) and the Sunflower Star (*Pycnopodia helianthoides*). Species such as the deep-water Bubblegum Coral (*Paragorgia arborea*) demonstrate that our cold waters harbour life and ecosystems as exquisite and precious as those in tropical seas. Bubblegum Coral further illustrates that ancient old-growth communities occur not only on land but in the sea. It grows only two centimetres per year to a maximum height of two metres. Elsewhere, cloud sponges grow into the best examples of globally unique glass-sponge reef ecosystems on the bare rocks in the frigid fjords of our province.

BC's geologically active sites have also provided surprises as far as invertebrates go. Hydrothermal (hot water) vents occur on the seafloor in association with plate tectonic activity. Deep in the ocean these underwater chemical chimneys support unique sea tubeworm (Vestimentiferan) communities that depend on chemical energy rather than sunlight. Specimens of these are in our collections.

As with insects, new species continue to be discovered on a regular basis. Over the years several new sea-cucumber species have been added on the basis of our comprehensive collections. The powerful techniques of molecular biology are helping to reveal the

FACING: Gavin Hanke, curator of vertebrate zoology, with some Dall's Sheep skulls, among the 100,000 vertebrate specimens in the collection. Hanke's specialty is fossilized fish.

richness of our marine fauna. Recently a new species of deep-water clam was described from our waters. Its scientific name, *Ascetoaxinus quatsinoensis*, honours Quatsino Sound on northern Vancouver Island, where it lives.

Our invertebrate collections and studies also help reveal much about the relationship between humans and the marine environment. The Olympia Oyster (*Ostrea lurida*) was once widespread along our coast and may have even been cultivated in intertidal rock impoundments called "clam gardens" by First Nations communities. But intense harvesting, beginning with the west-coast gold rushes in the late 1850s, drastically reduced its populations by the 1930s. Most people forget that such creatures even existed. Known historically as "Olys" these oysters are now a species of special concern and much effort is being put into restoring their habitat and numbers.

The museum's invertebrate collections and research continue to promote a better understanding and improved stewardship of our coastal waters.

Animals with Backbones

Visitors to natural history museums often come face to face with large stuffed mammals—bears or deer—posed amid artificial vegetation. The stuffed specimens in the Royal BC Museum's natural history dioramas always attract attention.

Specimens of the Kermode Bear came to us in the early 1900s, one of which became the type (or original reference) specimen. A century ago the discovery of this bear caused quite a stir of interest and controversy—was it a separate species or a subspecies or neither? When biologists determined that it was simply a colour variation of American Black Bear (*Ursus americanus*), the white bear retired from the stage of human curiosity—until the last decade, when the Kermode bear acquired a new name, "Spirit Bear," and it became the symbol of the coastal rainforest, its image leading the campaign to save this globally precious ecosystem. You can see Spirit Bears in movies and on the internet, and if you're really lucky you'll see one in the wild. But the original specimens that started it all still reside in our collections.

At the opposite end of the size scale, remarkable discoveries are being made in the world of shrews. You might think that, with the small number of mammals in BC (compared, say, to bees), finding or recognizing new species would be impossible. Yet since the 1960s, mammalogists have nearly doubled the number of shrew species, from seven to thirteen. Four of these, such as the Tundra Shrew (*Sorex tundrensis)* of extreme northwestern BC, are exceedingly rare and finding it was simply a matter of more looking. Another group, including the Dusky Shew (*Sorex moniticolus*), has turned out to be more diverse, as revealed by studies of its DNA. Ongoing investigations of specimens at the museum are trying to link visible features of the skull with the DNA differences in the animals.

Zoology

It can be said that one small vertebrate, the Southern Red-backed Vole (*Myodes gapperi occidentalis*), helped save a globally unique wetland. Not seen since the 1940s, specimens of this palm-sized creature were discovered in 1999 during scientific studies of Burns Bog in the Lower Mainland and deposited at the museum. The occurrence of such a rare creature in the bog added much weight to the initiative to save this unique ecosystem, which was purchased through contributions by all levels of government. It now stands as a world-renowned example of raised bog conservation and restoration.

Fishes are vertebrates, too, and they have obviously played a vital role in our province's economy and traditional life ways. Curator of Vertebrates Gavin Hanke estimates that 450 species of marine fishes inhabit BC waters. A remarkable 10 per cent of this number has been discovered within the last 15 years. Re-examination of specimens in our collections, and donations from the museum's collaborators in Fisheries and Oceans Canada and through the Marine Fisheries Observer Program, have added 44 new species.

Our vertebrate research and collections starkly demonstrate the changing composition of the province's ecosystems. The museum holds the first collection of European Wall Lizards (*Podarcis muralis*) made in BC. These brightly coloured characters brought here from southern Europe seemed to have survived in rock walls on a single property on the Saanich Peninsula after a small family zoo closed in 1970. They made front-page news in Victoria's daily

FACING: A drawer full of specimens of owls, among the 450 bird species in the museum.

newspaper as their populations began to expand, still hugging those warm sunny walls. Forty years later, these lizards can be seen darting across roads, playgrounds and fields throughout Greater Victoria. How they will affect our native species and ecosystems we do not know yet. But you can be sure the museum will have a collection documenting this example of an invasive vertebrate species for future scientists to study.

Into the Future

Museums and museum collections are often thought of as musty old places, monuments to and repositories of the past. Indeed, a critic once wrote that our *Climate Change* exhibition did not belong in our galleries because it speculated on possible futures. This view that museums should only be concerned with the past is erroneous and outdated for all of our collections, especially those of natural history.

I study microscopic pollen grains and their abundance in lake sediments spanning thousands of years, hardly the stuff of great exhibit halls. I and a colleague at Simon Fraser University have studied cedar pollen (mostly Western Redcedar, *Thuja plicata*), tracking its history since glacial ice left our province, and published the results in the respected journal *Science*. We showed that Western Redcedars only became widespread when modern climate arose about 4,000 years ago. The world-renowned cultures and lifeways of Northwest Coast aboriginal peoples flourished after this increase in Redcedar abundance. We demonstrated the strong connection of human cultures with nature, one might even say its dependence. In this time of crisis of sustainability, this lesson in itself is important for the future.

The lessons did not end with this discovery. From looking at cedar pollen records in western North America I realized that Western Redcedar, with its need for a moderate, moist climate, is an excellent bio-indicator—a rather large canary in a coal mine, so to speak—of the potential impacts of global climate change. After all, the climate shapes the physical and biological landscape, as the fossil record so clearly tells us. Accordingly I suggested that if our cedars were to decline in health and even die off, we might be seeing the first clear impact of climate change. Now, 20 years later, Western Redcedars in climatically dry regions, such as the east side of Vancouver Island, are in serious decline. A long-time museum docent recently came to me and reflected that I had foretold the future. Of course not, I replied; I had simply used the knowledge gained from some of the most insignificant pieces of our collections and applied it to one of the most pressing issues of the day.

As this example shows, natural history collections and research at the Royal BC Museum—at any museum—have enormous potential to inform and enlighten us, to stimulate deep thought and help us face challenges in British Columbia and around the world. Museums are not custodians of the past. They hold the keys to a better future.

Above Okanagan Lake, 1960, by E.J. Hughes. Hughes is best known for his highly detailed, almost naïve coastal scenes, and this painting of the semi-arid Okanagan Valley is a rarity in his oeuvre.

The Black Tusk, Garibaldi Park, a 1934 oil painting by J.W.G. "Jock" Macdonald, one of Canada's leading modernist—and later abstractionist—painters. A volcanic remnant just south of the resort town of Whistler, the Black Tusk is a striking landmark for skiers and hikers, and for motorists driving north from Vancouver.

NEXT PAGE: This finely carved and polished stone figure, from the interior of British Columbia, was used in ritual activity over 1,000 years ago.

GRANT KEDDIE

WHERE WE'VE BEEN AND WHO WE ARE

THE ARCHAEOLOGY COLLECTIONS

L-M
A-D
Keddie File
Historical Documents
R-S
Keddie File
Historical Documents
T-Z
E-K
Keddie File
Historical Documents
Songhees References
N-Q
Keddie File

FACING: Grant Keddie, curator of archaeology, using a stone tool he made himself to shape an arrow shaft.

ABOUT 16,000 YEARS ago the great migration of humans across the planet spread into what is now British Columbia. These people came with long-established histories and a knowledge base that enabled them to adapt to the many different environments they encountered. Some populations remained here, while others eventually moved further south. The ones who stayed left behind evidence of their activities: massive shell middens; scattered stone flakes where a hunter made tools while watching for game; a tree with bark removed for making baskets; a rock carving of a killer whale; posts from a fish weir exposed by a shifting river mouth; a large, strangely shaped boulder that is the focus of a First Nations story passed down through the generations.

It is this evidence that archaeologists at the Royal BC Museum collect and preserve. What we collect and how we collect it have changed over time with the development of the science of archaeology and the involvement of First Nations in revealing their longer history. Artifacts described as "Indian curios" in the early 20th century have become evidence for First Nations land claims in the last few decades. Archaeologists in the late 1960s focused solely on the chronological sequencing of artifacts, which then gave rise to examining the significance of those artifacts in the wider context of their environment. Collections started to include: faunal remains to provide us with details of what people ate; soil and feature samples that identified activities such as pit baking; charcoal samples for dating; site maps; more extensive field notes, excavation forms and photographs; and petroglyph rubbings and casts.

Working Together

First Nations are increasingly working with archaeologists on hundreds of projects every year. The Royal BC Museum is the main provincial repository for material coming out of these projects. Some First Nations are now developing their own repositories and a few have their own archaeology departments. To many First Nations, archaeology reinforces their link to the landscape. The recording of archaeological sites and the excavation of those that contain buried deposits provide not only stories of their history, but also evidence that can be used in land claims. Connection with the land is important in establishing personal and cultural identity.

Archaeology gives us a sense of who we are by helping to reveal where we have been. In British Columbia, it has helped many First Nations cultures and individuals discover their rich history, which was not part of their formal education. Some First Nations who want to understand their traditional cultures have been limited by having to interpret them through a buffer created by several generations of Christian teachings. They often struggle to reach a compromise by blending what they see as their traditional religion with those of the European world. The more earthly cultural heroes—the tricksters and transformers who changed the world to the way it is—are often interpreted through the filter of the Christian tradition, where they take on the characteristics of the Christian god.

Many First Nations, especially the younger generations, embrace archaeology as a method of discovering who they are, as a provider of evidence of their rich history. The artifacts uncovered by archaeologists are not just things to them, but part of a past that contributes to their identity. Artistic artifacts provide symbolic expressions of the nature of earlier cultures that attract the attention of modern First Nation artists who wish to reinvigorate those older expressions—at least in their design.

Respect for Human Remains

Some of the most artistic expressions of the past are found in artifacts associated with human burials. First Nations today have developed procedures that enable them to deal with the dilemma of how one maintains the proper respect for human burials and the need for cultural enhancement. Some want human remains and anything found with them immediately reburied, while others want to study artifacts before a formal reburial takes place. One First Nation decided to make replicas of burial goods and restrict the use of the originals after reburying the remains in the traditional respectful manner. Some First Nations regard archaeologic remains as things intentionally revealed by the ancestors and the discoveries as events that were meant to happen to form a cultural connection between the living and the dead. Others have taken DNA samples of their people and compared them with samples from ancient remains found in their traditional territory—participants in a comparative study of DNA on the northern coast have found that their ancestors have lived in the same area for the last 5000 years.

From the 1890s to the 1950s human remains were brought to the provincial museum by various police forces or government officials who did not know what else to do with them. First Nations at the time were only concerned with human remains that were from known cemeteries and not ancient remains. In the 1970s human remains deemed to not be of forensic concern were sent to the Archaeology Branch of the provincial government. The branch sent a letter to the closest First Nation in the area of the find and asked them what they wished to do with the remains. If the First Nation did not respond to the letter within six months, the branch's policy was to send the remains to the museum to be "held in trust for the band." Some First Nations responded but were not ready to make a decision at the time and asked that the remains be held by the provincial museum until they could respond with instructions. Other archaeological remains ended up at the museum because of agreements with First Nations.

The museum's policy regarding human remains held in stewardship for First Nations was to return them upon receiving a letter from the chief and council of a legally constituted band. In the 1990s it returned the majority of human remains that it had held in trust for various bands.

The process of returning remains then slowed down due to the development of the treaty process, which resulted in numerous overlapping claim areas. Remains could only be returned to areas where there was no overlapping claim or if all the parties involved agreed who should receive them. The Royal BC Museum no longer accepts human remains, but turns over any reports of found remains to the local police and coroner's office.

Goals of Archaeology

In British Columbia, one of the major goals of archaeology is to understand how groups of people developed and changed their culture in response to a changing environment, with other human beings forming an important part of the environment. Archaeologists throughout the world ask this question in order to make comparisons and gain a broader understanding of

FACING: This beautiful Elk antler comb, dating to 1400 years ago, was found in an archaeological site in Esquimalt Harbour on Vancouver Island.

human cultures in general. The goals of First Nations with regard to archaeological work are still developing and changing. One of them is to study land use as a basis for land claims and resource-use agreements.

Most archaeological information lies not in museums but still buried in the ground. This fact provides greater opportunities for First Nations, archaeologists and the Royal BC Museum to work together in recording, preserving and presenting the long and rich history of First Nations in this province.

Future Options

First Nations will increasingly acquire appropriate repositories to maintain the integrity of information and material collections. Future options will depend on the nature of the collections from specific areas. They may include sharing in the stewardship of the artifacts from their prescribed claim areas, making custodial agreements for information sharing, and setting special conditions regarding the acceptance of material to other local or larger regional repositories such as museums or universities.

Preserving History

The provincial government has an interest in preserving the cultural heritage of all peoples in British Columbia. Part of that heritage exists in archaeological information, which includes written and visual data and material objects. Visual data may come in the form of photographs, field notes and maps. Material objects may be artifacts made of stone, bone, antler, shell and—when preserved under special conditions—wood, as well as soil samples, animal remains and plant remains.

This information is used by different people for different purposes. One person may be inspired by the work of an ancient artist, another to bring about an appreciation of cultural groups by emphasizing their knowledge and technical skills. The more formal scientific use of archaeological information is to tell the story of humanity in this portion of the world. Scientists reconstruct patterns of settlement, resource use and human interaction in the past. Larger sets of information are used to reconstruct past lifeways at points in time, to look for and identify those important cultural processes that make cultures the way they are, or to examine the broader picture in the reconstruction of cultural history.

There are many subsets of material objects that can be used for an endless variety of studies. Animal bones, especially through DNA and isotope studies, become a source of information to help us understand the history and ecology of modern species.

Most people who use archaeological information place too much emphasis on artifacts, which are really only one component. Artifacts can, of course, be viewed individually as objects of study or aesthetic admiration, but to study them in an archaeological context, to understand their true meaning, they must be seen as part of an assemblage of information coming from a part of the landscape.

The existing laws protecting archaeological sites, and the undertaking of archaeological work, are primarily for scientific study. The data collected and prepared at archaeological sites—including maps, photographs, drawings, field notes, soil samples, artifacts and food remains in the form of animal bones and plant parts—constitute evidence of past lifeways. This evidence contributes to continuing research that builds a much broader picture of past cultures, and becomes a source of inspiration and learning for the present. Further studies undertaken at the museum add more data to the collection.

A great deal of effort and money has been put into collecting and studying this material over the years. It is important to maintain the scientific integrity of these collections.

Public Use of Collections

The archaeology collection also has great value as a source of information for public programming and artistic endeavours. Objects and visuals of an archaeological nature may be used as part of the explanatory framework in larger concepts, where they represent things or ideas.

Most of the scientific information associated with an object or group of objects is compiled during the collection and report-writing process. But an important value of collections lies in follow-up studies

FACING TOP: Spindle whorls, made of stone or sea mammal bone, were used to spin fibres for making string and yarn.

FACING BOTTOM: Polished slate club of a type used in warfare over the last 900 years.

and in comparison studies with other archaeological collections. Access to this information is important to maintain the scientific usefulness of the collections. More kinds of follow-up studies will be possible as our ideas and technological abilities evolve.

What are the Archaeological Artifact Collections?

This museum began acquiring archaeological material in 1886 under the Provincial Museum Act. The archaeology collection currently comprises over 225,000 catalogued artifacts representing up to 11,000 years of history. Artifacts include objects of First Nation, Euro-American, European and Asian manufacture, but 99 per cent are related to First Nations cultures. Collections include mostly stone, bone and shell artifacts, as well as other smaller categories such as wood, minerals and metals. The vast majority of stone (or *lithic*) artifacts are pieces of broken objects and waste material discarded in the production of tools and other objects. More complete stone artifacts are mostly related to the procurement and processing of food and include what archaeologists call retouched flakes, bifaces (implements flaked on both surfaces) and projectile points. Bone and antler artifacts are mostly from less acidic coastal shell middens and include a large number of bone fragments of unknown use, worked waste material, and fragments of tools used in fishing, hunting and the fabrication of plant or fur materials. Social artifacts include mostly stone and shell beads but also rarer items of body adornment or carved items of artistic interest.

The collection also contains hundreds of petroglyph (rock-carving) rubbings on cloth, and casts and moulds of artifacts. It has about 100 linear metres of artifact catalogue records, archaeological site records, field records, maps and research data, and thousands of associated photographs. Off-site archaeological collections include several thousand boxes of archaeological material, including animal bone and shell samples, charcoal samples for radio-carbon dating, various types of matrix and soil and column samples from archaeological excavations, and moulds and casts of petroglyphs.

Provincial Distribution of Collections

Over 70 per cent of the artifacts in the Royal BC Museum's archaeology collection are from southern BC (coast and interior), which has been occupied historically by speakers of the Salish language family. This is largely because most disturbance to the landscape occurs in areas with the highest populations, and because most archaeological work is done where urban, industrial or other development takes place. More than 90,000 artifacts in our collection are from the lower Fraser River region south of Lytton and the southern two-thirds of Vancouver Island.

There is a distinct south-to-north decline in the number of artifacts found in the province. More than 128,000 artifacts (about 45 per cent) of the collection come from below 50°N latitude. The number drops to

FACING: Heavy stone pile driver used for pounding wooden stakes into riverbeds for the attachment of fish traps.

around 75,000 artifacts between 50° and 52° and to 15,000 between 52° and 54°. Only about 7,000 artifacts (3 per cent) of the collection have been found in the northern half of the province, north of 54°N.

Collecting History

During the provincial museum's first 74 years—from the 1880s until the early 1960s—there was no professional staff with specialized training in archaeology. The collection was composed of mostly non-scientifically collected artifacts donated by the public. Then, in the mid 1960s and 1970s, museum archaeologists collected more and more artifacts along with large quantities of related excavation material.

The 1960 Archaeological Sites Protection Act and its 1972 replacement, the Archaeological and Historic Sites Protection Act, included the development of a permit system that requires archaeologists throughout the province to place the materials and information from their archaeological projects in a repository for safekeeping that is also accessible for scientific research. The Royal BC Museum has been the main provincial repository for material collected under permit since 1960.

With the gradual reduction of museum staff with archaeological training from ten in the mid 1970s to only two since 2000, museum projects have generated fewer and fewer collections. Most archaeological material entering our collection since the mid 1980s has been deposited by private contractors operating under the provincial permit system. With archaeological contractors working over wider areas, the collections are becoming more representative of the province, but the bias toward the south coast continues. This preference for the southwest persists due to ongoing development in more highly populated areas and because even in ancient times larger populations inhabited southern areas of the province, so sites in that region contain larger quantities of artifacts, faunal remains and other associated materials.

Cultural Strengths and Weaknesses of the Collection

The Royal BC Museum's archaeology collection contains more artifacts than any other collection of its kind, many representing a type or style not found in any other collection.

The strongest part of the collection is the large sampling of study material from the southern portion of the province over the last 3,000 years. Almost every item in the collection has a site-number designation and about 95 per cent is entered into a computer database with varying levels of information. About 20 per cent of the items in the collection needs its data corrected and updated.

This collection is the most valuable source of information documenting the early history of First Nations in British Columbia. The wide variety of research that can be undertaken on this collection will form the basis for both academic and public discussions about First Nations in this region for many years to come.

OVERLEAF: Details of two images from "The Moody Album," a gold-rush era book containing some of the earliest photographs taken in BC; left: Colonel Richard Moody, an official, with Lieutenant Anderson; right: Moody with an unidentified First Nations man.

GARY MITCHELL

A TREASURE TROVE HIDDEN IN PLAIN VIEW

THE BC ARCHIVES

FACING: "Tait-tots-toe," a Tsehaht man, photographed around 1868.

FOR MORE THAN 100 years, the historical documents, maps, sound recordings and films documenting the history of our province and its communities have been held at the British Columbia Archives. The collection of our provincial archives is a precious treasure, although it is often the silent partner in documentary films, history books and articles, public presentations, exhibitions in museums and art galleries, and historical novels. This archives, like other archives, is dedicated to the accessibility and preservation of our history and heritage for today's citizens and for each successive generation.

When I speak of the BC Archives, I refer to the collections of historical records, maps, drawings, films and tapes, and so on, and not to the organization or the buildings that house them. After all, the collections will long outlive any structure that holds them and any bureaucratic organization that manages them.

FACING: *Church at Yale*, a painting from 1930 by Fred Varley, a founding member of the Group of Seven who was deeply inspired by the coastal landscape of British Columbia.

The official opening of the BC Archives was in 1908, the 50th anniversary of the founding of the colony of British Columbia. But the collecting of publications and manuscripts, diaries, photographs and other records relating to European and Canadian presence in British Columbia had begun a decade earlier. The newly established legislative library, the research library of British Columbia's government, began collecting, through a public appeal, publications and historic materials and this formed the basis of the famed Northwest collection, with its editions of Captain James Cook's voyages in multiple European languages, the Ortelius atlas and similar historical documents.

British Columbian society in the 1890s and first decades of the 20th century was growing in self-confidence and seeking to solidify its historical presence, so it was eager to collect information about the pioneering families and early governments of the old colonies (Vancouver Island and British Columbia) and the young province. At this time in British Columbia, there were no universities or colleges, no city or community museums or archives, and no museum of history. The Provincial Museum of Natural History and Anthropology, founded in 1886, devoted itself to collecting specimens and artifacts related to natural history and ethnography. There was a void.

Through the actions and drive of Legislative Librarian R.E. (Edward) Gosnell, the store rooms and attics of government were searched for early records, a copying program of early BC records in Westminster and Ottawa was begun and, of course, the public appeal for donations was issued. Gosnell became the first provincial archivist. He sought to collect and document the early era of British Columbia. Unlike any of his successors, Gosnell had many political connections and used his clout to heighten the need to collect historical materials.

In the early 20th century the first books on BC history were published, and soon afterward the first formal history societies and associations were formed to promote and educate the young province on its history. The archives took up residence in the legislative buildings alongside the provincial museum and the legislative library. This proximity gave the archives an aura of importance. The provincial archivist was not only a founding member of an emerging history society but now had a key leadership role.

The early years of the collection saw the inevitable realization that simply collecting material did not support public access to the archives, even in a limited capacity. Methods of description and access were desperately needed to make the collections available to researchers. The years leading up to and including World War I saw limited growth in the archives, as with other public services.

The Great War had a profound impact upon BC communities—many towns did not survive it, as so many young men did not return to resume their labours. But with its end came the awakening (or at least the recognition) of a unique Canadian identity. In 1921,

10

as British Columbia celebrated the 50th anniversary of its entry into Confederation, the British Columbia Historical Association was founded from the many smaller community history groups, and shortly thereafter, the newly created Historic Sites and Monuments Board of Canada designated its first sites in British Columbia. Within this historic fervour, the BC Archives began collecting diaries, maps, images and other material from the outlying communities to ensure that the historical record of the pioneering generation was protected. For the next 50 years, until the centennial celebrations of the founding of the colony of British Columbia, the BC Archives remained the only archives in BC documenting the history and heritage of the former colonies and the early province (except for the City of Vancouver Archives, which is dedicated only to the preservation of Vancouver's history).

Archives are *open* institutions—places where anyone can study the historical record. In the 1920s researchers had to make an appointment at the BC Archives, in part due to there being no catalogues or finding aids to support their research, and only a small number of archivists to locate the records for them. From the 1930s onwards, as more archival records were classified and made available, researchers began to enjoy greater access. The research community at that time was primarily historians, authors, students and others with a keen interest in the province's history; the general public did not visit archives as they did museums, as part of one's cultural experience. It would be many decades yet before archives became part of the common heritage experience.

FACING: Kathryn Bridge, deputy director of the BC Archives, in the painting collection. The archives contains about 10,000 paintings, drawings and prints of British Columbia, more than half of which can now be viewed digitally.

Photographs and paintings have been part of the BC Archives' collection strategy since it was founded. In the years before photography became commonplace, paintings were often the way people recorded the world around them. The BC Archives has collected some extraordinary works of art, both for their artistic value and their documentary value (for example, the work of Sophie Pemberton).

Records kept by the early European and Canadian families who settled in BC—such as the O'Reillys of Victoria, the Robinsons of Peachland and the Bayliffs in the Chilcotin—document the early society and government life in the colony.

The world of archives continued relatively unchanged through the Depression, World War II and into the early post-war era. British Columbians, like all Canadians, were rebuilding. During this period W. Kaye Lamb served as provincial archivist from 1933 to 1941. Lamb was one of the first people with a doctorate hired by the BC government and he later became Dominion archivist and national librarian of Canada. He must be regarded as one of our nation's greatest historians and authors. Lamb famously coined the phrase: "Any country worthy of a future should be interested in its past."

In the mid 1950s British Columbia began its preparations for three centennial celebrations: the centennial of the founding of the colony of British Columbia (1958), the centennial of the union of the colonies of British Columbia and Vancouver Island (1966) and the centennial of BC's entry into the Canadian Confederation (1971). The celebrations would touch every region and community in the province. Public facilities, such as swimming pools, community halls, museums and archives, were funded as centennial projects. Barkerville, the famed gold-rush town, was saved from ruin and designated as a historic site, as was the Hudson's Bay post at Fort Langley, the site of the proclamation of the colony of British Columbia. The province went all out to celebrate its history and showcase its energy and vitality as an emerging part of Canada.

Much like 50 years earlier, the celebrations inspired great interest among the citizens of BC in their history. The BC Archives underwent a growth spurt that saw its expansion into the collection and preservation of audio tapes, film and colour photography. Agreements with the Reynoldston Research project (an oral history project gathering the histories of the Great War and Depression generation) and the Canadian Broadcasting Corporation created one of the first audio and film archives in the country.

This expansion was not the only major change. The centennial celebrations had invigorated community pride in local, provincial and national heritage. While Canadian studies programs emerged at the universities and colleges, the majority of archives' clientele shifted from historians and academics to writers of popular local histories and researchers seeking information about communities and families.

Staffing and resources at the BC Archives increased in 1970 to support the move from the cramped legislative buildings into the new Heritage Precinct site (where it still resides). The precinct project itself was a federal and provincial centennial project and reflected the significance of heritage to both governments and to Canadians in general. Community archives were also being established throughout the province. The BC Archives, no longer the only collector of archival records in BC, helped guide and mentor these smaller archives.

The shift in users and the new demands for access to photographs, video tapes and audio tapes brought to the forefront the need for national standards for access, description and acquisition. BC Archives staff members were among the leaders in creating national description standards, especially with film and audio media. These standards were adopted nationally and led the way in establishing international standards.

As the decade of the 1970s closed, the BC Archives had become the largest archives west of Ontario. It was noted for its collection of colonial and pioneering records, its oral history and film collection, and its photographic collection. Its research library rivalled the major universities in its collection of British Columbian cultural materials and associated publications for Alaska and Spanish California. Its collection of colonial and provincial government records was impressive, but there remained no organized method of deposit within government and its agencies.

Notable records collected during this time included:

- Reynoldston Research oral collection: This collection of more than 500 tapes consists of interviews pertaining to the histories of BC trade unions, the University of British Columbia, various ethnic groups in BC and the roles of women.
- Imbert Orchard collection: Orchard's documentary history program at the CBC includes 71 audio cassettes, 51 audio tape reels, about 900 other audio recordings, 2 film reels and 305 photographs.

In the 1980s the federal and provincial governments in Canada undertook major cost-saving measures. British Columbia, especially, saw major shifts in public services, and although the BC Archives was not adversely affected by cuts in resources and personnel, its focus began to shift away from collecting historical records in communities to concentrating on the historical records of government.

In 1988 the archives merged with the recently established records management program and supervised the implementation of standardized records-keeping systems in government agencies, including standardized records storage and archival deposit by authorized schedules.

For the next 15 years, the BC Archives concentrated primarily on the collection of historical documentation from government departments. Thousands of metres of records were emptied from government filing cabinets and storage rooms and placed into secured storage centres, where archives staff began sifting through

Archivist Raymond Frogner studying one of the discs recorded by ethnomusicologist Ida Halpern; one of her recording devices can be seen on page 42.

them to separate those of long-term value (that is, evidentiary, legal and historical value) for safekeeping.

Concentration on this massive undertaking curtailed the collection of records from individuals, families and companies. Indeed, the collection of non-government records became so passive that many community archives considered it non-existent. This public perception makes it impossible to calculate how many of these records were not offered to the BC Archives and other archives—we will simply never know.

The clientele of the BC Archives continued to grow and was now firmly transformed from a predominantly academic base to one of community and family history researchers, forming two-thirds of the users. As one would expect, the new user base wanted better access to the audio and film archives and to photographic collections. The reference room, with its wood panels and banks of catalogue cards, saw a greater emphasis on microfilm readers and audio and video stations, as researchers viewed and listened to the newest archival records.

The archives also began moving its reference service into the emerging world of the internet. It rebranded its reference services as *access services* to acknowledge the changing environment of research demands and expectations. Archives and archivists were moving from being the *gatekeepers* of history and heritage toward the *stewards* of the collections.

As stewards, archivists were now responsible for explaining historical context and assisting in deciphering colonial or provincial government processes and policies to researchers. The BC Archives was one of the first Canadian archives to place its entire finding aids to the collection online and one of the first North American archives to place historical vital statistics (births, deaths and marriages) online. Its partnership with the BC Vital Statistics Agency on the release of its historical information was one of the first projects to highlight the research potentiality of the internet.

As the millennium closed, the BC Archives, like many archives, were facing higher researcher demands

The Lee family immigrated to British Columbia from China around 1900; they used the family portrait below as a greeting card for Christmas 1911.

for broader access to historical records and more online access to all archival information. It also encountered preservation challenges as the audio and film holdings began showing signs of deterioration. Much has been written on how the internet and global search engines have democratized the world; one of the most impacted heritage agencies has been archives.

As an open institution, archives now received demands for greater access, faster response times and a larger online presence. The researcher community and the general public began to view archives as a place where citizens could hold their elected and government officials to account for themselves. Researchers no longer visited the archives reference room to pore over ledgers and files—they demanded digitized material sent to their homes. On-site visits and the traditional in-person meetings with archivists were decreasing. The definition of "open" now extended to unfiltered archival access.

The challenges associated with public demands for greater access and the growing realization that significant conservation efforts would be needed to protect and preserve the audio and visual archives as well as late-20th-century paper archives, along with the cost of digitalization, were exacerbated by the provincial government's reductions in financing for archives and heritage agencies.

Although the emphasis on keeping government records curtailed acquisitions, several major collections highlight the phase:

- Courthouse and Judicial Records Project: Over the course of 15 years, the historical records of the courthouse were identified, documented and transferred to the BC Archives.
- Government Information Services: A collection of thousands of images documenting government activities from the 1950s to the 1980s, including the first use of colour photography in government.
- BC Forest Service Collection: A photographic collection documenting the influence of the Forest Service across the regions, as well as an extensive collection of environment images.

The Current State

On April 1, 2003, the provincial government merged the BC Archives and the Royal BC Museum into a new Crown corporation called the Royal BC Museum. For the first time in its history, the BC Archives had legislation outlining its function. This legislation eliminated the archives' role in government records keeping and re-instituted a private-acquisitions program (collecting the records of individuals and companies).

The renewed emphasis on acquiring private records was reinforced with the support of the curators and collection managers of the museum's history department. The renewed emphasis on collecting outside of government inspired efforts to reach out to the province's diverse minority communities and to establish trusting relationships, which will eventually see the deposit of historical records from community associations, families and businesses. The combined museum and archives makes it possible to display archival records with artifacts in a great variety of exhibitions. The archives' "silent partner" character of decades past is being set aside with each history exhibit and display showing archival material alongside museum artifacts and specimens.

The BC Archives' researcher base continues to broaden. Indeed, demands and expectations from researchers have continued to rise as new social media technologies encourage faster and faster response times. The demand for more and more online resources poses new challenges, not only in making the material available, but also in describing the content and context of the historical record.

As part of its stewardship role and growing demands for digital online material, the archives has conducted risk-assessment studies and identified which archival records are in peril. Most recently, the audio and film archives have been placed into either cool or cold storage in order to preserve the physical media as well as the information embedded upon them. In these cases, digitalization may be the only preservation method. Of course, once digitized, the material is available online and the original material can be safely returned to cold storage.

This refreshed approach has brought several deposits to the BC Archives, including:

- Pemberton Realty: The business records from one of the longest-running real-estate companies in western Canada document the growth of urban British Columbia and reveal how a multi-generation company has survived for over a century.
- *The Lantern:* Not just an artifact of import, the *Lantern* illustrates the contributions of families in Victoria toward settling political unrest in China and the surviving ties of the oldest Chinatown in Canada to their ancestral homeland.

What of the Future?

True to its foundations of a century ago, the BC Archives continues to collect and preserve the historical records of British Columbia and make them accessible to the public.

Like all archives today, the BC Archives is adapting to the digital age. A great challenge awaits as all heritage groups, museums, archives and galleries try to find common standards for maintaining the authenticity and integrity of electronic records of historical value. Do we maintain outdated hardware and software programming to provide access? Do we incorporate conversion routines to consistently bring forward historical data? The questions, at this time, remain unanswered.

But great opportunities abound for archives. The electronic technologies have brought immediacy to the accessibility of historical information.

The integration of the provincial museum and archives in 2003 could not have foreseen the potential for bringing forward historical information and records into the daily lives of our society. The BC Archives, like other archives, has shifted from a source location of primary documents to an active integrated location where public accountabilities can be reviewed and analysed, and where public forums and discussions can be heard on historic issues related to current hot topics.

Future plans for a research centre with archival and public programming components fit perfectly into this emerging world. Access to archival records will be available to researchers and the general public everywhere at any time. Virtual access to exhibits, public programming, public presentations, curatorial sessions and public forums, with its seamless use of archival content, will focus on the ever-increasing public demand for verifiable and authentic historical information.

Although virtual visits to the archives' research centre will outpace on-site visits, the nature of on-site research will require specialized examinations of the historical records' formats and content, with stronger contextual support. Part of these examinations will include access to "decision" documents of elected and government officials. This is the new world of forensic archival research and will require specialized training for archives staff.

The research centre gives the BC Archives and Royal BC Museum a focal point to further establish the trust relationships with our diverse minority communities to allow for the safe transfer of their records before the passing of the direct descendants of the arrivals generation. Virtual exhibitions and presentations enable us to illustrate and illuminate the importance of these communities to the fabric of BC society.

For those interested in re-creating or restoring elements of our past, ever-increasing access to archives will continue as part of its daily business. The use of audio tapes and historic images in a live theatre presentation on logging is an example in the arts. Another prime example of the use of archival information to support and aid in the restoration of a historic site is the use of the BC Archives by Stefan and Magda Opalski in their restoration of the 1863 Wentworth Villa, one of the few remaining Carpenter Gothic-style houses in Victoria.

For the BC Archives, the observance of key milestones has always been advantageous to its mission. Within the next decade, British Columbia and Canada will commemorate the centennial of the Great War and the Battle of Vimy Ridge—a cornerstone of our national identity and a key battle for British Columbian military units; we will also celebrate the 150th anniversary of Canadian Confederation and the 150th anniversary of BC's entry into Confederation. The BC Historical Federation, an association that the early BC Archives guided and mentored, will celebrate its centennial in 2022. From these milestones, our society will, once again, hold its historical legacy and continuance of its heritage to a higher degree of importance. It is the perfect time to cast a light on our archival treasures and bring them forward with the new technologies.

NEVERSWEAT

NOTES

Travelling by Carr

1 Emily Carr, Letter to Nan Cheney, February 7, 1932. Quoted in Doris Shadbolt, *The Art of Emily Carr* (Vancouver: Douglas & McIntyre, 1979), p. 180.

2 Emily Carr, "Ucluelet," *Klee Wyck* (Toronto/London: Oxford University Press, 1941), p. 3.

3 Carr, "Skedans," *Klee Wyck*, p. 29.

4 Nootka is not only the name of the place. It was once the name given to the First Nations who live along the west coast of Vancouver Island, now known as Nuu-chah-nulth. In their book *The Whaling People of the West Coast of Vancouver Island and Cape Flattery* (Victoria: Royal BC Museum, 2011), Eugene Arima and Alan Hoover explain how the name Nootka arose "from Captain James Cook mistakenly thinking that the large inlet he visited in 1778 was called 'Nootka'. Gesturing, he asked some native men what the place was called. The men did not understand him but guessed that he wanted to know if the inlet continued around the large island, and with a circling gesture supposedly replied ... *'Nootksheeee! Nootkshiʔe ch'aʔakʔee!'*, meaning 'Get round! Get around the island!', warning Cook about the reefs he was approaching at Yuquot village." Pp. 5–6.

5 Neil Bissoondath, "Continental Drift," *Digging Up the Mountains* (Toronto: Macmillan, 1986), p. 146.

6 Bissoondath, p. 147.

7 Ben Stiller plays Larry, the night watchman in a large New York museum, in the movie *Night at the Museum* (2006).

8 The immigrant mix in towns like Yale and Barkerville and their complicated relations with First Nations groups (not least the Fraser River War of 1858) is examined by historians such as Daniel P. Marshall. See, for instance, "Mapping the New El Dorado: The Fraser River Gold Rush and the Appropriation of Native Space" (2007), reprinted in *Interpreting Canada's Past: A Pre-Confederation Reader*, 4th edition, edited by J.M. Bumsted et al. (Toronto: Oxford University Press, 2011), pp. 406–21.

9 See also pages 56–57 in this book.

10 Carr, "D'Sonoqua," *Klee Wyck*, p. 52.

11 In the Haida language this village is called *t'anuu 'llnagaay*, meaning "eelgrass town."

FACING: Miners at the Neversweat Tunnel Claim near Williams Creek, about 1868. The photo is by Frederick Dally, see pages 38 and 40.

Living Cultures

1 Douglas Cole, *Captured Heritage: The Scramble for Northwest Coast Artifacts* (Vancouver: Douglas & McIntyre, 1986), p. 133.

2 See Martha Black, "The Heiltsuk Case: Museums, Collectors, Inventories" (PhD dissertation, University of Victoria, 1998).

3 See Black, "The Heiltsuk Case."

4 "Curios of Savage Life," *Daily Colonist*, Victoria, April 15, 1893, p. 6.

5 Newcombe Family Papers, BC Archives MS-1077, series A, volume 4, folder 86.

6 Cole, *Captured Heritage*, pp. 63–64.

7 Peter Corley-Smith, *White Bears and Other Curiosities: The First 100 Years of the Royal British Columbia Museum* (Victoria: Royal BC Museum, 1989), p. 43.

8 Cole, *Captured Heritage*, pp. 229–30.

9 Dan Savard, *Images from the Likeness House* (Victoria: Royal BC Museum, 2010), pp. 114–24. For a discussion of photography and ethnographic collection, see Martha Black, "Display and Captures: Some Historic Photographs from the Northwest Coast," *American Indian Art Magazine* 18 (Winter, 1992), pp. 68–75.

10 British Columbia Provincial Museum *Annual Report* (Victoria: British Columbia Department of Education, 1953).

11 British Columbia Arts Society, *Mungo Martin, Man of Two Cultures* (Sidney: Gray's Publishing, 1987).

12 For an expanded discussion, see Martha Black, "Collaborations: A Historical Perspective," in *Native Art of the Northwest Coast: A History of Changing Ideas*, edited by Charlotte Townsend-Gault, Jennifer Kramer and Ki-ke-in (Vancouver: UBC Press, 2013), pp. 785–827.

13 Ronald W. Hawker, *Tales of Ghosts: First Nations Art in British Columbia 1922–61* (Vancouver: UBC Press, 2003), pp. 177–78.

14 Wilson Duff, *Histories, Territories and Laws of the Kitwancool*, Anthropology in British Columbia Memoir No. 4 (Victoria: British Columbia Provincial Museum, 1959; reprinted 1989), p. 3. This book has been in print for more than 50 years.

15 Richard I. Inglis and Donald N. Abbott, "A Tradition of Partnership: The Royal British Columbia Museum and First Peoples," *Albert Museums Review* 17:2 (1991), p. 20.

16 Duff, *Histories, Territories and Laws of the Kitwancool*, p. 12.

17 Ira Jacknis, *The Storage Box of Tradition: Kwakiutl Art, Anthropologists and Museums, 1881–1981* (Washington, DC: Smithsonian Institution Press, 2002).

18 Jacknis, *The Storage Box of Tradition*, p. 215.

19 Martha Black, "What the Treaty Means to Us: Museums and Treaties in British Columbia," in *Northwest Coast Representations: New Perspectives on History, Art and Encounters*, by Andreas Etges, Viola König, Rainer Hatoum and Tina Brüderlin (Berlin: Dietrich Reimer Verlag GMBH, in press).

ABOUT THE AUTHORS

Jack Lohman has been chief executive officer of the Royal BC Museum since 2012. He has vast experience working with international cultural institutions. From 2002 to 2012, Jack was Director of the Museum of London, where he led the redevelopment of the Galleries of Modern London. From 1999 to 2002 he was CEO of Iziko Museums of Cape Town, an organization of 15 South African museums. He is a board member and former Chairman of the National Museum in Warsaw, Poland, professor in Museum Design and Communication at the Bergen National Academy of the Arts in Norway and Editor in Chief of UNESCO's publication series *Museums and Diversity*.

Jack Lohman has received honorary doctorates from the Universities of Westminster, London (PUNO) and East Anglia. He was awarded the CBE in 2012 and the Bene Merito Medal for services to Poland in 2011, and was honoured by the prime minister of Rwanda in 2010 for his services to Rwanda. His most recent publication is *Museums at the Crossroads? Essays on Cultural Institutions in a Time of Change.*

Martha Black has been curator of ethnology at the Royal BC Museum since 1997. Before coming to the museum she was Curator and Associate Director of The Isaacs Gallery in Toronto. Martha has worked on many collaborative projects with First Nations and is a specialist in the theory and practice of repatriation within and outside of the treaty negotiation process. She has curated a number of exhibitions at the Royal BC Museum and published two books: *Out of the Mist: Treasures of the Nuu-chah-nulth Chiefs* and *Bella Bella: A Season of Heiltsuk Art.*

Richard J. Hebda is curator of botany and earth history. He has been with the Royal BC Museum since 1980, and since 1984 has also held faculty positions at the University of Victoria's Department of Biology and School of Earth and Ocean Sciences. His PhD in botany is from the University of British Columbia. Richard's areas of study include plant fossils, ethnobotany of BC First Nations, restoration of natural systems and processes, botany of grasses and alpine ecosystems. He has written or co-written more than 120 scientific papers, 250 popular articles and eight books and major reports. He is the province's expert advisor on Burns Bog and science advisor on paleontology.

Grant Keddie has been curator of archaeology at the Royal BC Museum for 42 years. He combines an extensive knowledge of the archaeology collection with his interest in human history and natural history. His studies look at human behaviour in the past by examining the changes in the archaeological and ethnographic records. A popular speaker and demonstrator, Grant has carried out archaeological work across the province and published on a wide range of topics, including the ethno-history *Songhees Pictorial: A History of the Songhees People as seen by Outsiders, 1790–1912.*

Gary Mitchell is provincial archivist, emeritus. He holds a master's degree in archival studies and became a manager with the BC Archives in the late 1980s. He became provincial archivist in 1998 and retired in July of 2014 as vice president, archives, collections and knowledge.

I WISH TO THANK friends and associates for their contributions: Richard Hebda and Martha Black, who gave many helpful suggestions to me at the outset of the project; Gary Mitchell and Grant Keddie, who helped me shape the final presentation; and my collaborators on the practical aspects of pulling together the book, Erika Stenson and Erik Lambertson. I should particularly like to mention Gerry Truscott, who masterfully edited these contributions, and the book's outstanding creative managing editor Scott Steedman and designer Peter Cocking. I am also immensely grateful to our superb photographer, John Sherlock, who intuitively understood each object's power. —JACK LOHMAN

Published by the Royal British Columbia Museum
675 Belleville Street
Victoria BC Canada V8W 9W2

Library and Archives Canada Cataloguing in Publication

Royal BC Museum, issuing body
Treasures of the Royal British Columbia Museum and Archives / compiled by Jack Lohman; with contributions from Steven Point, Martha Black, Richard J. Hebda, Grant Keddie, Gary Mitchell.

Includes bibliographical references.
ISBN 978-0-7726-6830-1 (bound).

1. Royal BC Museum—Catalogues. 2. British Columbia—Civilization—Catalogues. 3. British Columbia—History—Catalogues. 4. Natural history—British Columbia—Catalogues. I. Lohman, Jack, 1958–, editor II. Point, Steven, writer of supplementary textual content III. Title.

AM101.V5153R698 2015 971.10074′71128 C2015-900120-X

All photography of museum staff, exhibits and artifacts by John Sherlock, except for: pages 12–13, 21, 93, 94, 103, 106, 110, 117, 119 (both), 120 by Shane Lighter; page 91 by Andrew Niemann; pages 30, 98 by RBCM staff photographers. All photography of artworks by RBCM staff photographers. Archival photographs by John Wallace Jones or Thomas McNabb Jones (11); Frederick Dally (38, 138); Carl Günther (53); Richard Maynard (57); Travel Bureau (68); Barratt's Photo Press Ltd. (69); unknown Royal Engineer photographer (122, 123); Charles Gentile (126); Larrigan (134); unknown photographer (10, 44).

OPENING IMAGES:

pp. 2–3, detail of the argillite chest attributed to da.a xiigang, Charles Edenshaw, shown in full on p. 73

p. 4, detail of the Chinese Freemasons' lantern shown in full on p. 124

p. 5, detail of the poem in Chinese shown in full on p. 41

p. 6, view of Chinatown in Old Town

p. 7, detail from *Industry,* a two-part mural of dockyard and railway workers in Vancouver, by Orville Fisher, Paul Goranson and E.J. Hughes, 1939. A larger version of this mural was one of 15 sent by the province to the Golden Gate International Exposition in San Francisco, California.

p. 10, felling a cedar tree by hand, date unknown

p. 11, photographic portrait, possibly of the man known as Tyee Jim, about 1897

p. 14, scale model of q'una 'llnagaay (the Haida village of Skedans) in the *First Peoples* gallery

p. 15, Grizzly Bear in the coastal forest diorama

p. 18, view of the *Our Living Languages* exhibition

p. 22, detail of a Kwakwa̲ka̲'wakw house post in Wawadit'ła (Mungo Martin House), Thunderbird Park, showing Dzunuk'wa (a mythical wild woman), a crest of the K̲wik̲wa̲sutinux̲w people of Gilford Island

p. 23, cover of one of the Douglas Treaties, shown in full on p. 32

p. 24, detail of *Sombreness Sunlit* by Emily Carr, 1939–40